McGRAW-HILL READING

Grammar

Grade 1

Practice Book

McGraw-Hill
School Division

New York   Farmington

CONTENTS

Book 1.2: Together Is Better

Book 1.3: Stories to Tell

Book 1.4: Let's Find Out!

Book 1.5, Unit 1: Think About It!

Book 1.5, Unit 2: Many Paths

Sentences

- A **sentence** is a group of words.

- A **sentence** tells a complete thought.

> A **sentence**:
> Max likes to nap.
>
> **Not a sentence:**
> Naps in a cap.

Circle the sentences.

1. Max hugs Pam.

2. A mat and a cap.

3. Max naps and naps.

4. Max likes Pam.

5. A nap on the mat.

EXTENSION: Have the children use complete sentences to tell about their own pet or a pet they would like to have.

I

Sentences

- A **sentence** is a group of words.
- A **sentence** tells a complete thought.

Sentences:	Not sentences:
Pam has a cat.	Pam's cat
Max is the cat.	is the cat

Read each group of words. Circle the sentence that tells a complete thought.

1. Pam has a cap.

2. Pam likes the cap.

3. Max naps in the cap.

4. a nap in the cap.

5. Pam gives Max a hug.

6. Pam's cat Max.

EXTENSION: You may have the children make up a sentence about places for pets to nap.

Writing Sentences

- A **sentence** is a group of words.
- A **sentence** tells a complete thought.

Look at the picture and the words in the box.
Make the words tell a complete thought.
Write the sentence.

a mat	to help	Pam	Max

1. Pam has _____.

2. Max wants _____.

3. _____ sits on a mat.

4. _____ sees Pam on the mat.

EXTENSION: Write incomplete sentences on the chalkboard. Have the children complete them.

Sentences

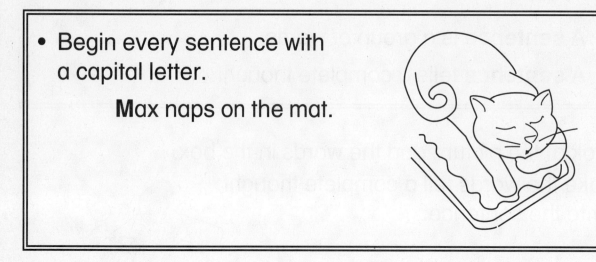

- Begin every sentence with a capital letter.

    Max naps on the mat.

Read the words.

Draw a circle around the capital letters.

Draw a line under words that are <u>not</u> a sentence.

1. Max cannot nap in this cap.

2. Pam is sad.

3. a mat for a nap.

4. Pam gives the cat a hug.

5. Pam's cat.

McGraw-Hill School Division

EXTENSION: Have children compose sentences about pets and dictate them for the teacher or assistant to write on a chalkboard or chart.

Book 1.1
Max the Cat

 5

Sentences

Circle each complete sentence.

1. a cat on a mat

Pam has a mat.

Max in a cap

2. Pam likes Max.

Pam's mat

Pam and Max

3. cat on a mat

Max has

Max is a cat.

4. Pam's nap

Max naps in a cap.

mat for a nap

5. Pam gives Max a hug.

Max's mat

a hug is

Sentences

- A sentence is a group of words.
- A sentence tells a complete thought.
- Every sentence begins with a capital letter.

Read the sentences about each picture. Write the sentences correctly. Make a sentence if the group of words does not tell a complete thought.

I. max is a cat.

_____

- - - - - - - - - - - - -

_____

2. Pam's cat.

_____

- - - - - - - - - - - - -

_____

3. max likes to sleep.

_____

- - - - - - - - - - - - -

_____

4. Max sleeping.

_____

- - - - - - - - - - - - -

_____

Word Order in Sentences

- Words in sentences have to tell a complete thought.

    I pack my hat.

- The words have to be in the right order.

    I help pack.

- These words are <u>not</u> in the right order.

    help pack I

Draw a circle around the sentences with the words in the right order.

1. van the That is

2. This is Dad.

3. They pack the van.

4. I my bat. pack

EXTENSION: You may have the children reorder the words to make sentences out of those that are incorrectly ordered.

Word Order in Sentences

- The words in a sentence have to be in order.

    I pack my bat.

- The order has to make sense.

    I pack my cap on my bat.

- This order does <u>not</u> make sense.

    I map pack my

Read the words.

Draw a circle around the words that make sense.

1. Quack. not Do pack

2. Do not pack Quack.

3. Mack Jack. and Good-bye,

4. Quack is in the van.

EXTENSION: Have the children place the words that do not make
sense in correct order. Then have them check their sentences to
be sure that they have capital letters at the beginning.

Book 1.1
Quack! 4

McGraw-Hill School Division

Word Order in Sentences

> - The words in a sentence have to be in the right order.
> - The order has to make sense.

These words are not in order.
Write the words in order.

1. the Pack van.

_____

- - - - - - - - - - - - - - - -

_____

2. pack and Jack Mack.

_____

- - - - - - - - - - - - - - - -

_____

3. Dad pack and Jack.

_____

- - - - - - - - - - - - - - - -

_____

4. in the van Quack is.

_____

- - - - - - - - - - - - - - - -

_____

EXTENSION: Have the children write sentences. Then have them mix up the word order. Exchange with a classmate and put the words back in order.

Word Order in Sentences

> • A sentence ends with a special mark.
>
>   Quack is in the van.

Put the words in order.
Write the sentence.
End it with a special mark.

1. packs Jack

_____

– – – – – – – – – – – – – – – – – – –

_____

2. van the Dad packs

_____

– – – – – – – – – – – – – – – – – – –

_____

3. in van the Quack is

_____

– – – – – – – – – – – – – – – – – – –

_____

4. packs Dad Quack

_____

– – – – – – – – – – – – – – – – – – –

_____

EXTENSION: Have the students write sentences about
moving pet animals. Then have them show where the period
belongs.

Book 1.1
Quack! | 4

Word Order in Sentences

Read each sentence.
Find the words that complete the sentence.
Circle the words that complete the sentence.

1. Dad packed the _
van.
Jack.
the.

2. Do not pack _
Pack.
Quack.
help.

3. Jack helps _
van.
the.
Dad.

4. Mack can _
help Dad.
help can.
and can.

5. The duck _
do my.
and Jack.
is in the van.

Word Order in Sentences

- Words in sentences tell a complete thought.
  Dad helps Quack.
- The words must make sense.
  Quack a help Dad ← **(Does not make sense.)**

Mechanics:
- End every sentence with a special mark.
  Quack can help Dad.

Write the words in order. Write the mark at the end.

1. packs Jack

_____

- -

_____

2. I Dad help

_____

- -

_____

3. pack I will

_____

- -

_____

4. van Quack is in the

_____

- -

_____

5. Mack Jack and the pack van

_____

- -

_____

McGraw-Hill School Division

Statements

> • A **statement** tells something.
>   This is a **statement**.
>   Pig picks a wig.

Find the **statements**.
Draw a circle around the **statements**.

1. Pig digs.

2. Pig kicks.

3. Pig

4. Pig taps and bats.

5. Laps

---

5 | Book 1.1
What Does Pig Do?

EXTENSION: You may have the children tell statements about
the things they do on the different days of the week. These
could be whole class or small group activities.

Match Statements with Pictures

- A **statement** tells something.

    I see a pig.

Draw a line from the statement to its picture.

1. Pig naps.

2. Pig kicks.

3. Pig has a wig.

4. Pig digs

EXTENSION: You may have the children work in groups composing statements about the things they like to do on Sundays. They can make pictures to go with their statements.

Writing Statements

> • A **statement** tells something.
>
>   Pig has a bat.

Write a statement about each picture.

1._____

2._____

3._____

McGraw-Hill School Division

EXTENSION: Have children work together to write statements. Write the statements on a chalkboard or chart.

Statements

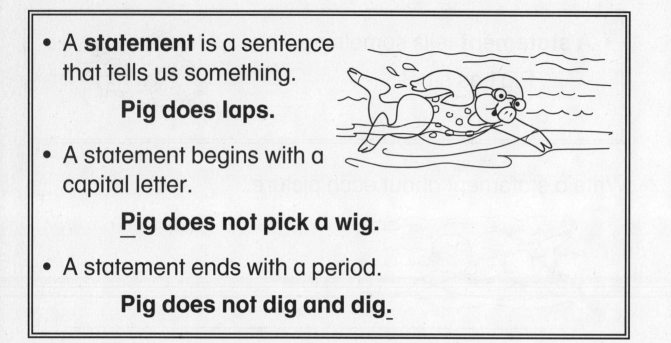

- A **statement** is a sentence that tells us something.

  Pig does laps.

- A statement begins with a capital letter.

  Pig does not pick a wig.

- A statement ends with a period.

  Pig does not dig and dig.

Circle the words that should have a capital letter.
Put a period at the end of each statement.

1. pig does not kick and kick

2. pig does not tap and tap

3. pig does swim

4. not kick

5. pig does nap

EXTENSION: Have children compose statements about the things they do not do on Sunday. Have them include capital letters and periods.

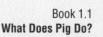

McGraw-Hill School Division

Statements

Read the words.
Draw a line under each statement.
Circle each capital letter.
Circle each period.

1. Pig does not do laps.

taps

not do

2. not do

Pig has a bat.

kicks is

3. on do

Pig does not tap and tap.

laps on

4. Pig does nap.

not does

tap and

5. not kick kick

pig not

Pig does not kick and kick.

Statements

- A statement is a sentence that tells something.
- Begin a statement with a capital letter.
- End a statement with a period.

Look at each picture. Read the words. Circle the letter that should be a capital letter. Put a period at the end.

on Monday, Pig picks a wig

on Friday, Pig bats

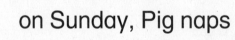

on Sunday, Pig naps

Write a statement about the things you do on Sunday.

_____

_ _ _ _ _ _ _ _ _ _ _ _ _ _ _ _ _ _ _ _

_____

Questions and Exclamations

- A **question** is a sentence that asks something.

   Can you see the pig?

Read the sentences.
Find the **questions**.
Circle the questions.

1. Can you see it?

2. A fat cow is on this map.

3. Can you see the duck?

4. A fish is here.

5. Can you see the pig?

EXTENSION: Have the children change the statements to questions.

Questions and Exclamations

> • An **exclamation** is a sentence that shows strong feelings.
>
> **Look out! A cat is in the shack!**

Read the sentences. Circle the exclamations.

1. More cats are in the shack!

2. That is a big, big fish!

3. Can you see a fat cow?

4. What a happy day this is!

5. Can you see a pig on the map?

EXTENSION: Have children work in groups to compose exclamations about surprising or exciting events.

Book 1.1
The Path on the Map

McGraw-Hill School Division

Questions and Exclamations

> - A question is a sentence that asks something.
>
>   **What is on the map?**
>
> - An exclamation is a sentence that shows strong feeling.
>
>   **That is a big, fat cow!**

Read the sentences.
Circle the questions.
Draw a line under the
exclamations.

1. Can you see the fat cow?

2. Why is a duck on this map?

3. That is a big fish!

Write a question about the big fish.

_____

_ _

_____

Write an exclamation about the cat in the shack.

_____

_ _

_____

5 Book 1.1
The Path on the Map

EXTENSION: Have the children compose exclamations and questions.
Match them with partners. Have them say their sentences aloud, so their
partners can say whether the sentences are questions or exclamations.

End Marks for Questions and Exclamations

- A **question** ends with a question mark.

  Can you see the big duck?

- An **exclamation** ends with an exclamation mark.

  That is a big cat!

Read the sentences.
Write a question mark at the end of the questions.
Write an exclamation mark at the end of the exclamations.

1. Can you see the path

2. Look at that big cat

3. I like cats

4. What could be in the shack

5. That shack is not on the map

EXTENSION: Have the children think of sentences that are questions or exclamations. After they say their sentences aloud, their classmates can tell whether the sentence needs a question mark or an exclamation mark.

Book 1.1
The Path on the Map

5

McGraw-Hill School Division

Questions and Exclamations

Read each sentence.
Circle the correct end mark for each sentence.

1. Do you have a map

    .   !   ?

2. This path is long

    !   ?   .

3. That is a big, big fish

    ?   .   !

4. What could be in the shack

    ?   !   .

5. Look out for the cats

    !   .   ?

Questions and Exclamations

- A **question** is a sentence that asks something.
- End a question with a question mark.
- An **exclamation** is a sentence that shows strong feeling.
- End an exclamation with an exclamation point.

Read each sentence aloud. Put the question marks and exclamation points at the end.

1. What is on this map

2. Can you see it on the map

3. That is a big, big fish

4. I see more and more cats

5. What can I do with the cats

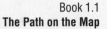
McGraw-Hill School Division

Writing Sentences

- Every **sentence** begins with a capital letter.

  Look at the ship.

- A **statement** ends with a period.

  Look at the big ship.

- A **question** ends with a question mark.

  Do you like the ship?

Write a statement about the picture. Write a capital letter at the beginning and a period at the end.

1. this is a steam ship

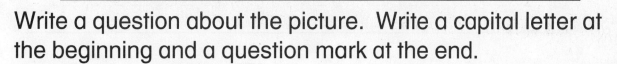

_____

_ _ _ _ _ _ _ _ _ _ _ _ _ _ _ _ _ _

_____

Write a question about the picture. Write a capital letter at the beginning and a question mark at the end.

2. is this a Navy ship

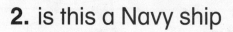

_____

_ _ _ _ _ _ _ _ _ _ _ _ _ _ _ _ _ _

_____

McGraw-Hill School Division

Book 1.1
Ships

EXTENSION: Ask the class to identify whether the sentences are statements or questions.

25

Writing Sentences

- Every sentence begins with a capital letter.

  The little ship has sails.

- An exclamation ends with an exclamation mark.

  That is a big, big ship!

Write each exclamation on the lines. Write a capital letter at the beginning. Write an exclamation mark at the end.

1. look at that big ship

_____

_____

2. that is a big, big ship

_____

_____

3. look out for the small ship

_____

_____

McGraw-Hill School Division

EXTENSION: Have the children write exclamations. Ask them to explain why it is an exclamation, not a statement.

Writing Sentences

- A sentence begins with a capital letter.
    <u>I</u>t is a Navy ship.
- A statement ends with a period.
    The ship is big<u>.</u>
- A question ends with a question mark.
    Do you like big ships<u>?</u>
- An exclamation ends with an exclamation mark.
    This is a big ship<u>!</u>

---

1. Write a statement about a ship. Begin with a capital letter and end with a period.

_____

- -

_____

2. Write a question about a ship. Begin with a capital letter and end with a question mark.

_____

- -

_____

3. Write an exclamation about a ship. Begin with a capital letter and end with an exclamation mark.

_____

- -

_____

EXTENSION: Have the children work in groups and assign each group to compose a statement, a question, or an exclamation.

Writing Sentences

> • Begin every sentence with a capital letter.
>
> • End every sentence with a special mark.

Write the sentences. Write a capital letter at the beginning of every sentence. Write a period, an exclamation point, or a question mark at the end of every sentence.

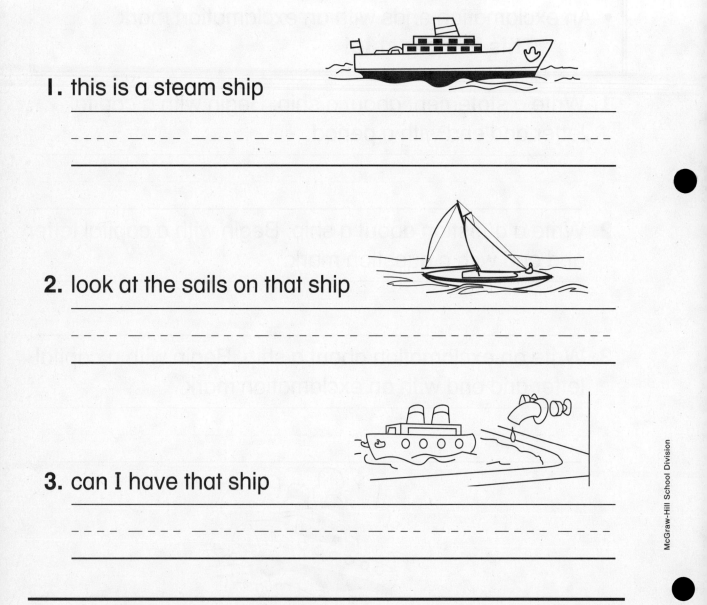

1. this is a steam ship

_____

_____

2. look at the sails on that ship

_____

_____

3. can I have that ship

_____

_____

McGraw-Hill School Division

EXTENSION: Have the children reread "Time for Kids" to find examples of capital letters at the beginning of sentences and of periods, question marks, and exclamation points.

Book 1.1
Ships

3

Writing Sentences

Write the end marks.

1. Look out for the big steam ship

2. Is the ship at sea

3. That is a big, big ship

4. Let's see the ship

5. Where is it

Write the capital letters.

6. _____ the ship is big.

7. _____ look out!

8. _____ do you see it?

McGraw-Hill School Division

Writing Sentences

> • Begin each sentence with a capital letter.
>
> • End a statement with a period.
>
> • End a question with a question mark.
>
> • An exclamation ends with an exclamation point.

Look at the picture. Read the sentences. Circle the
letter in each sentence that should be a capital
letter. Put the correct end mark.

1. what do you see

2. how many cats are there

3. pam likes cats

4. there are many kittens

5. the kittens like to play

Sentences

Read the sentences in the box. Look at the part with the line under it. Is there a mistake? How do you make it right? Mark your answer.

Max is a cat. <u>he likes to nap.</u> Max naps in a cap.
(1)

1. Ⓐ Begin with a capital letter.
   Ⓑ Put a period.
   Ⓒ Do not change.

Dad packs the van. <u>packs Dad Quack.</u> Quack is in the van.
(2)

2. Ⓐ Put a period.
   Ⓑ Put the words in order.
   Ⓒ Do not change.

<u>Pig bats.</u> Pig kicks and taps. Pig naps.
(3)

3. Ⓐ Put a period.
   Ⓑ Put the words in order.
   Ⓒ Do not change.

A cow is on this map. <u>Do you see it</u> It is a fat cow.
(4)

4. Ⓐ Put a period.
   Ⓑ Put a question mark.
   Ⓒ Do not change.

Go on

Look out Do you see the ship? That is a big, big ship!
(5)

5. Ⓐ Put a question mark.
Ⓑ Put an exclamation point.
Ⓒ Do not change.

I don't see a ship. where is it? There it is!
(6)

6. Ⓐ Begin with a capital letter.
Ⓑ Put a question mark.
Ⓒ Do not change.

Pig does not pick a wig. Pig does not bat. What does Pig do?
naps Pig!
(7)

7. Ⓐ Put the words in order.
Ⓑ Put a question mark.
Ⓒ Do not change.

What can I pack? I can pack my cap Watch out! There's a cat
in the cap!   (8)

8. Ⓐ Begin with a capital letter.
Ⓑ Put a period.
Ⓒ Do not change.

Nouns

> • A **noun** is a word that names a person, place, or thing.
>   The **dog** is big.   **Dog** is a noun.

Circle the nouns that name a person, an animal, or a thing.

1. The cat is black.

2. The boy has a toy.

3. The apple is red.

4. The mouse eats corn.

EXTENSION: Have the children name the things in the classroom. Point out that these names are called nouns.

Match Nouns with Pictures

> • A **noun** is a word that names a person, place, or thing.
>
> A **man** is a person.   **Man** is a noun.
>
> A **home** is a place.   **Home** is a noun.
>
> A **ship** is a thing.   **Ship** is a noun.

Draw a line from the sentence to the noun named in the sentence.

I. It is a wig.

2. We have a map.

3. This is a small ship.

4. This is my yard.

5. See the star.

EXTENSION: Have the children tell sentences about a toy they like (a thing). Then have them draw pictures of the toy.

McGraw-Hill School Division

Nouns in Sentences

> - A **noun** is a word that names a person, place, or thing.
> - A **noun** can name a place.
>
>   I will play at **home**.

Write the name of a place from the word box in the sentence.

| home | sky | hill | bank | yard |

1. I go _____ after school.

2. The _____ is blue.

3. The tree is on top of a _____.

4. I plant flowers in our _____.

5. I keep money in a _____.

EXTENSION: Have the students tell sentences that are about a place. Then have them draw pictures to show the place they told about.

Sentences

> • Begin each sentence with a capital letter.
> • End every sentence with a special mark.

Circle the sentences that are correct.

1. The cat is in the tub.

2. is there a fish in the tub

3. the map has a path

4. Pup wants to go out!

5. Pig has a wig.

McGraw-Hill School Division

EXTENSION: Divide the children into pairs. Have the children correct the incorrect sentences.

Nouns

Circle each noun that names the picture.

1. The dog is playing.

2. A girl is reading.

3. The owl hoots.

4. The kite flies.

5. Go to the top of the hill.

6. It is a big house.

Nouns

> • A **noun** is a word that names a person, place, or thing.
> • A **noun** can name a place.

Mechanics:
• Begin each sentence with a capital letter.
• End every sentence with a special mark.

Circle the nouns. Write the sentence correctly.

I. see the toy in the tub

_____

- -

_____

2. i have a big cat

_____

- -

_____

3. the dog is in the yard

_____

- -

_____

4. find the path on the map

_____

- -

_____

5. look at the duck

_____

- -

_____

EXTENSION: Divide the children into pairs. Assign each pair to tell a sentence about a person they know, a place they like, or a thing they see in the classroom.

Book 1.2
One Good Pup   5

McGraw-Hill School Division

Plural Nouns

- Some nouns name **more than one person, place, or thing**.
- This kind of noun is called a **plural noun**.
- Add **-s** to make most nouns name more than one.

  one bug ➔ two bugs

Circle the plural nouns.

1. Two girls are talking.

2. The mittens are warm.

3. Three birds flew.

4. Ducks swim in a pond.

EXTENSION: Have the children write the plural nouns they circle on the chalkboard or on writing paper.

Plural Nouns

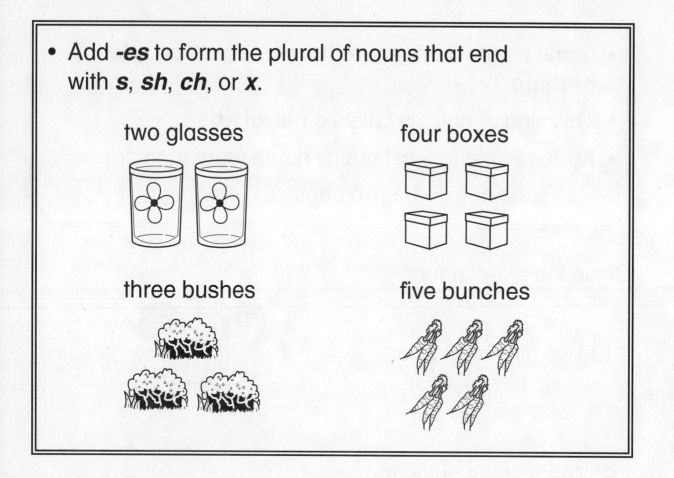

- Add **-es** to form the plural of nouns that end with **s**, **sh**, **ch**, or **x**.

two glasses

four boxes

three bushes

five bunches

Circle the plural nouns.

1. The bushes are wet.

2. Two buses were at the bus stop.

3. Let's have hot lunches.

4. See the red foxes.

5. Two classes are going.

EXTENSION: Write wish, church, and pass on the chalkboard. Have the students make them plural.

Book 1.2
The Bug Bath

5

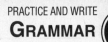
Match Plural Nouns with Pictures

- Add **-s** to make most nouns name more than one.

    The <u>bugs</u> fell in the tub.

- Add **-es** to form the plural of nouns that end with **s**, **sh**, **ch**, or **x**.

Read the sentences. Find the plural nouns.
Draw a line from each sentence to the picture of the
noun that added **-s** or **-es**.

I. I see two houses.

2. The dishes are on the table.

3. See the three churches.

4. Pack the toys in boxes.

5. I have two cats.

6. There are two foxes.

 Book 1.2
The Bug Bath

EXTENSION: Have the children reread stories in their
readers and locate plural nouns.

Sentences with Plural Nouns

> - Begin every sentence with a capital letter.
> - End a question with a question mark.

Read the sentences.
Circle each word that should have a capital letter.
End a question with a question mark.
Add **-s** or **-es** to the noun if it names more than one thing.

1. the four duck quack.

2. Can I pack two box

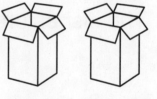

3. are those ladybug

4. How many duck are in the tub

5. i have two pup .

McGraw-Hill School Division

EXTENSION: Have the children tell sentences that have
plural nouns. Then ask the children to tell which nouns
should end with *-s* and which should end with *-es*.

Book 1.2
The Bug Bath

5

Test

Read the sentences.
Find the plural nouns.
Mark the letter next to each plural noun.

1. The two _____ got in.

   Ⓐ bugs   Ⓑ cat   Ⓒ the

2. Three big _____ fell in the tub.

   Ⓐ a   Ⓑ ducks   Ⓒ not

3. Jack has four big _____ .

   Ⓐ car   Ⓑ can   Ⓒ glasses

4. Mack packs two _____ .

   Ⓐ boxes   Ⓑ the   Ⓒ one

5. The _____ are big.

   Ⓐ saw   Ⓑ churches   Ⓒ in

Plural Nouns

- Add **-s** to make most nouns name more than one.
- Add **-es** to form the plural of nouns that end with **s**, **sh**, **ch**, or **x**.

Read each sentence aloud. Write the plural noun.

1. The four ducks quack.

_____

_ _ _ _ _ _ _ _ _ _ _ _ _ _ _ _ _ _ _ _

_____

2. I can pack two boxes.

_____

_ _ _ _ _ _ _ _ _ _ _ _ _ _ _ _ _ _ _ _

_____

3. The bugs are in the tub.

_____

_ _ _ _ _ _ _ _ _ _ _ _ _ _ _ _ _ _ _ _

_____

4. I see three foxes.

_____

_ _ _ _ _ _ _ _ _ _ _ _ _ _ _ _ _ _ _ _

_____

5. Do you have two glasses?

_____

_ _ _ _ _ _ _ _ _ _ _ _ _ _ _ _ _ _ _ _

_____

EXTENSION: Have the children tell sentences that have plural nouns. Then ask the children to tell which nouns should end with -s and which should end with -es.

Book 1.2
The Bug Bath   5

McGraw-Hill School Division

Irregular Plural Nouns

- Some nouns that name more than one do <u>not</u> end with **-s**.

Singular	Plural
child	children
goose	geese
foot	feet
man	men
tooth	teeth
mouse	mice

Read the sentences. The chart and the pictures will help you find the nouns. Write the noun in the blank.

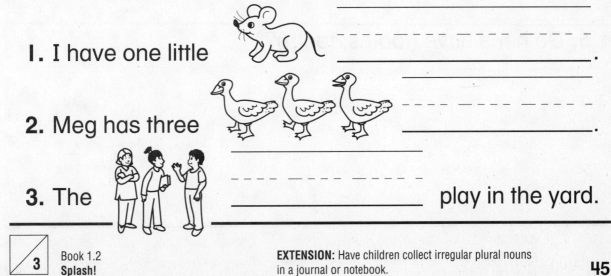

1. I have one little _____.

2. Meg has three _____.

3. The _____ play in the yard.

EXTENSION: Have children collect irregular plural nouns in a journal or notebook.

McGraw-Hill School Division

Irregular Plural Nouns

- Some nouns that name more than one do <u>not</u> end with **-s** or **-es**.

- These nouns are the plural forms of **child**, **goose**, **foot**, **man**, **tooth**, **mouse**.

Read the sentences.
Find the plural nouns.
Draw a circle around the plural noun that goes in the sentence.

1. It rained on the three (gooses, geese).

2. The cat ran after two (mouses, mice).

3. All of the (men, mans) had wet hats.

4. The (children, childs) had fun in the rain.

5. How many (feet, foots) does the hen have?

6. Do hens have (tooths, teeth)?

EXTENSION: Have the children work in pairs to compose sentences with irregular plural nouns.

McGraw-Hill School Division

Irregular Plural Nouns

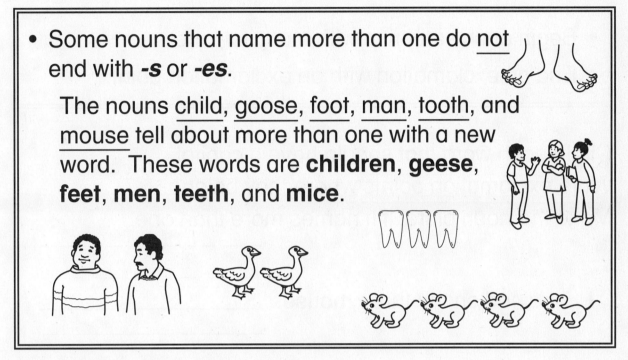

- Some nouns that name more than one do <u>not</u> end with **-s** or **-es**.

  The nouns <u>child</u>, <u>goose</u>, <u>foot</u>, <u>man</u>, <u>tooth</u>, and <u>mouse</u> tell about more than one with a new word. These words are **children**, **geese**, **feet**, **men**, **teeth**, and **mice**.

Read the nouns.
Write the plural for each noun.

child _____

goose _____

foot _____

man _____

tooth _____

mouse _____

EXTENSION: Write the singular nouns and the plural nouns on cards. Have the children play a game to match the cards. The pair or team that matches the most is the winner.

Sentences with Irregular Plural Nouns

> • Begin each sentence with a capital letter.
>
> • End an exclamation with an exclamation point.

Circle each word that should have a capital.
Write exclamation points where they belong.
Make the noun plural if it names more than one.

1. It rained on the three mouse. _____
_____
_____

2. it rained on the two goose. _____

3. the wet geese ran into the big red barn.

4. in the barn, they saw mice.

5. the geese did not like the mice.

6. See the mice run away

Book 1.2
Splash!

Plural Nouns

Circle the plural noun that should go in the sentence.

1. The three (goose, geese) had a bath.

2. Many (child, children) like to play.

3. Jack lost two (tooth, teeth).

4. The five (mouse, mice) like to nap.

5. Al has two (foot, feet).

6. The four (man, men) will make lunch.

McGraw-Hill School Division

Irregular Plural Nouns

> • Some nouns that name more than one do not
> end with **-s** or **-es**.

Look at the picture. Read the words next to it. Draw
a circle around the plural noun.

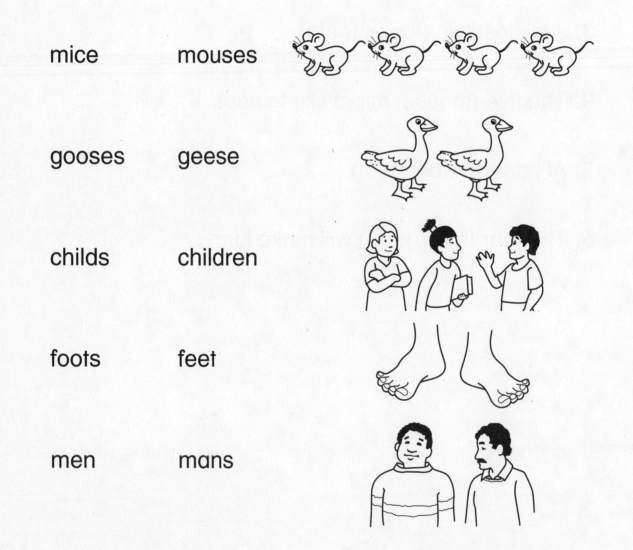

mice	mouses
gooses	geese
childs	children
foots	feet
men	mans

Proper Nouns

- Some nouns name a special person or place.
- This kind of noun is called a **proper noun**.
- A proper noun begins with a capital letter.

    Rick

Read the sentences. Find the proper nouns.
Draw a circle around the proper nouns that need a
capital letter.

1. rick saw a small bug.

2. "It is an ant!" said jill.

3. The bug walked on jas.

4. "That is a ladybug!" nell said.

5. yan saw a spider.

---

5 Book 1.2
What Bug Is It?

EXTENSION: Have the children write sentences using
their classmates' names as proper nouns.

51

Proper Nouns

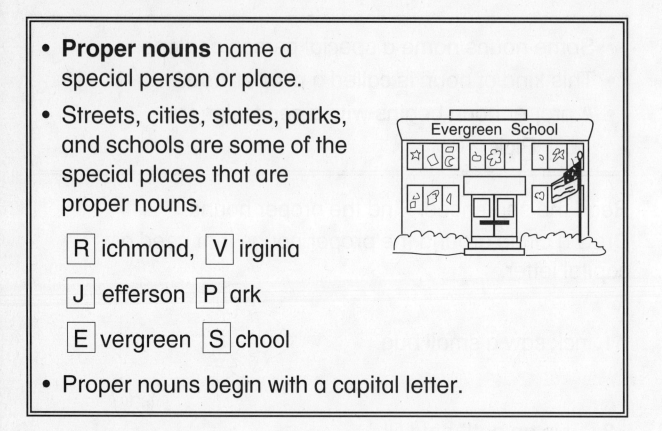

- **Proper nouns** name a special person or place.
- Streets, cities, states, parks, and schools are some of the special places that are proper nouns.

  Evergreen School

  R̲ichmond, V̲irginia

  J̲efferson P̲ark

  E̲vergreen S̲chool

- Proper nouns begin with a capital letter.

Read the sentences.
Draw a circle around the place names that need a capital letter.

1. Pam lives on elm street.

2. Rick's home is in new york.

3. There are big trees in grove park.

4. Max lives in ohio.

5. Jas goes to john adams school.

EXTENSION: Have the children compose sentences with the name of the city, town, or community where they live.

Book 1.2
What Bug Is It?

5

McGraw-Hill School Division

Proper Nouns

- **Proper nouns** name a special person or place.
- Proper nouns begin with a capital letter.

  P̲ am lives on S̲ pruce S̲ treet.

  J̲ ill's address is: J̲ ill M̲ ason

  124 P̲ leasant S̲ treet

  H̲ amilton, O̲ hio 42134

Write proper nouns that name people and places on the lines. Begin the names with capital letters.

My name is _____.

_____

My address is _____

_____

_____

_____

McGraw-Hill School Division

6 Book 1.2
What Bug Is It?

EXTENSION: Have the children compose sentences about local place names.

53

Proper Nouns

> • A proper noun names a special person or place.
>
> • A proper noun begins with a capital letter.

Read each sentence.
Circle the letters that should be capital letters.

1. "Look around," said miss Lin.

2. rick said, "I see a bug."

3. "I see a bug," said jill.

4. Nell goes to green school.

5. "It is a big bat," said yan.

Book 1.2
What Bug Is It?

 5

Proper Nouns

Read each sentence. Find the proper noun. Mark your answer.

1. We saw a spider at Green School.

   Ⓐ Green School

   Ⓑ We

   Ⓒ saw

2. "It will use its web to snag flies," said Miss Lin.

   Ⓐ It

   Ⓑ use

   Ⓒ Miss Lin

3. "It is a bee," said Jill.

   Ⓐ Jill

   Ⓑ a

   Ⓒ is

4. We saw bugs at Good Park.

   Ⓐ at

   Ⓑ We

   Ⓒ Good Park

5. "Let that bug pass!" said Jill.

   Ⓐ that

   Ⓑ Jill

   Ⓒ Let

Proper Nouns

> • Some nouns name a special person or place.
> • This kind of noun is called a proper noun.
> • A proper noun begins with a capital letter.

Read each sentence aloud. Draw a circle around
each proper noun.

1. Rick has a bug in a box.

2. Miss Lin sees a big cat.

3. Pam is in the yard.

4. Do you live in Texas?

5. Where is Spring Street?

6. I go to West End School.

Days, Months, and Holidays

- Some **proper nouns** name special people, pets, and places.
- **Proper nouns** begin with capital letters.
- Some **proper nouns** name the days of the week.
- The days of the week begin with capital letters.

  [S] unday   [M] onday   [T] uesday

  [W] ednesday   [T] hursday   [F] riday   [S] aturday

Write the day of the week on the lines.

Begin each day with a capital letter.

1. After Friday comes _____.

2. Before Tuesday comes _____.

3. The day after Wednesday is _____.

4. The day before Monday is _____.

5. After Thursday comes _____.

6. The day after Tuesday is _____.

Days, Months, and Holidays

- Some proper nouns name months.
- These proper nouns begin with capital letters.

Ⓙanuary, Ⓕebruary, Ⓜarch, Ⓐpril, Ⓜay, Ⓙune, Ⓙuly, Ⓐugust, Ⓢeptember, Ⓞctober, Ⓝovember, Ⓓecember

Read each sentence.
Draw a circle around the letters that need to be capitals.

1. School starts in august or september.

2. The first month is january.

3. My birthday is in june.

4. Valentine's Day is in february.

5. A hot month is august.

58

EXTENSION: Have the children name their favorite month and explain why it is their favorite. They can write a sentence about this month.

Book 1.2
A Vet

McGraw-Hill School Division

Days, Months, and Holidays

- Some proper nouns name holidays.
- The names of holidays begin with capital letters.
  Some of the holidays are:
  Thanksgiving   Christmas   New Year's Day
  Independence Day   Valentine's Day

Read the sentences.
Draw a circle around the holidays that need a capital letter.
Write the name of the holiday with a capital letter.

1. When is christmas?

_____

_ _ _ _ _ _ _ _ _ _ _ _ _ _

_____

2. We celebrate independence day
   on the fourth of July.

_____

_ _ _ _ _ _ _ _ _ _ _ _ _ _

_____

3. We are thankful on thanksgiving.

_ _ _ _ _ _ _ _ _ _ _ _ _ _

_____

4. We send cards on valentine's day.

_____

_ _ _ _ _ _ _ _ _ _ _ _ _ _

_____

4 Book 1.2
   A Vet

EXTENSION: Have the children tell how their family
celebrates a holiday. Then they can write a sentence
about the holiday.

Days, Months, and Holidays

- The name of each day begins with a capital letter.
- Monday, Tuesday, Wednesday
- The name of each month begins with a capital letter.
- March, April, May, June
- The name of a holiday begins with a capital letter.
- Mother's Day, Thanksgiving, Independence Day

Read the sentences. Write the days, months, and holidays. Give the days, months, and holidays capital letters.

_____

1. It rains in april. _____

_____

2. Summer begins in june. _____

3. thanksgiving is for giving thanks.

_____

_____

_____

4. monday is the first day in the week._____

5. On independence day, we have fun.

_____

_____

_____

EXTENSION: Have children write a sentence with a day and a month in it.

Book 1.2
A Vet 5

McGraw-Hill School Division

Days, Months, and Holidays

Read the sentences. Write the word that is correct.

1. We give thanks on _____.
thanksgiving   Thanksgiving

2. I go to school on _____.
Monday   monday

3. We give cards on _____.
valentine's day   Valentine's Day

4. My birthday is in _____.
may   May

5. I help Dad on _____.
Saturday   saturday

Days, Months, and Holidays

- Some proper nouns name days of the week.
- Some proper nouns name months.
- Some proper nouns name holidays.
- The name of each day begins with a capital letter.
- The name of each month begins with a capital letter.
- The name of a holiday begins with a capital letter.

Read the sentences. Put a circle on the letters that should be capital letters.

1. Meg has a birthday on wednesday.

2. Who has a birthday in may?

3. Will Al have a birthday in april?

4. Rick has a birthday on valentine's day.

5. I do not have a february birthday.

6. The vet gave me a dog in march.

Nouns

Choose the word that belongs in each space. Mark the letter for your answer.

I live in a __(1)__ on Main Street. It is a big house. My cat lives there too.

   1. Ⓐ house   Ⓑ cat   Ⓒ street

My cat is sick. Is the __(2)__ in?

   2. Ⓐ sick   Ⓑ vet   Ⓒ is

Our class will ride the bus. Two __(3)__ are going.

   3. Ⓐ bus   Ⓑ busss   Ⓒ buses

One duck swims away. Four __(4)__ quack.

   4. Ⓐ ducks   Ⓑ duckes   Ⓒ duck

It rained on one goose. Three __(5)__ ran into the barn.

   5. Ⓐ gooses   Ⓑ geese   Ⓒ goose

Go on

One mouse was in the barn. Three other ___(6)___ ran in with the geese.

6. Ⓐ mouses Ⓑ mice Ⓒ mouse

The barn is near Deer Park. The park is on Elm Street in El Paso, ___(7)___ .

7. Ⓐ Texas Ⓑ park Ⓒ town

We had a soccer game last Friday. Are we playing on ___(8)___ ?

8. Ⓐ Tuesday Ⓑ game Ⓒ soccer

My birthday is in December. When is your birthday? Is it in ___(9)___ ?

9. Ⓐ party Ⓑ June Ⓒ today

Grandma lives in Topeka, Kansas. She visits us every ___(10)___ .

10. Ⓐ airplane Ⓑ far Ⓒ Thanksgiving

Verbs

> • A **verb** is a word that shows action.
>
> Frog   **jumps**.
>   ↓
>   **verb**
>
> Owl   **blinks**.
>   ↓
>   **verb**

Read the sentences.
Draw a circle around the verbs.

I. Bat flips.

2. Stan's pals yelled.

3. "Stop it, Stan!"

4. Stan's pals hold their noses.

5. Frog and Stan jump.

Book 1.3
Stan's Stunt

EXTENSION: Have the children reread "Stan's Stunt" and find the verbs. Write the verbs on a chart for future reference.

Verbs

• A **verb** is a word that shows action.

I **draw** skunks.
↓
verb

You **sleep** in a tent.
↓
verb

Look at the pictures.

Find the stunts.

Draw a circle around the words that tell about the actions.

1. wagging   skunk   tail

2. jumping   frog   the

3. bird   singing   a

4. blinks   owl   the

5. dancing   cat   the

EXTENSION: Have the children think of stunts they could do for a show. Then ask them to make sentences about the stunts.

Book 1.3
Stan's Stunt

McGraw-Hill School Division

Writing Verbs in Sentences

> • A **verb** is a word that shows action.

Look at the picture. What actions do the animals do?
Write a verb in each sentence. Use a verb from the box.

| blink | jump | stop | flip |

_____

1. Frogs _____.

_____

2. Owl's lids _____.

_____

3. Bats _____.

_____

4. The animals _____ Stan.

Book 1.3
Stan's Stunt

EXTENSION: Have the children write sentences about
tricks they could do. Then have the other students find
the verbs in their sentences.

Commas in a Letter

- Use a comma after the greeting in a letter.

    Dear Grandmother,

- Use a comma after the closing in a letter.

    Love,

    Rick

Make a comma after each greeting. Make a comma after each closing.

Dear Kyle

I like to read. The bat in our book flips.

Your friend
Catherine

Dear Ann

We enjoy our stunts. We jump like frogs.

Your friend
Megan

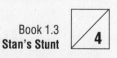

McGraw-Hill School Division

Test

Read the sentences. Circle the verbs.

1. I jump all day.

2. Owl's lids blink.

3. I see Owl's stunt.

4. Look at Stan's tail.

5. The animals stop Stan.

6. Stan and frog bump.

7. Draw the animals.

8. I read books.

More Practice with Verbs

> • A **verb** is a word that shows action.

Mechanics:
  • Use a comma after the greeting and the closing in a letter.

Find the verb. Write the verb to make a sentence.

_____

I. Stan _____.

the   jumps   red

_____

2. Owl _____.

blinks   on   frog

_____

3. Owl _____ with Frog.

stunt   plays   the

Put the missing commas in this letter.

Dear Stan
    Please stop your stunt.
                    Your friend
                    Frog

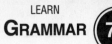
Present Tense

> • The **tense** of a verb tells when the action takes place.
>
> • Some verbs tell about actions that happen now.
>
> • These verbs are in the **present tense**.
>
> Greg **makes** a mask.
>
> Greg **sings**.

Circle the verbs that tell about actions that happen now.

1. Greg clips a mask.

2. Drop a glob of that.

3. Greg tossed it in the trash.

4. Twist it here.

5. Greg sang as he worked.

6. Pam loves her cat.

 Book 1.3
Greg's Mask

EXTENSION: Have the children think of sentences that tell the things they are doing. Write the present tense verbs they use on a chart.

Present Tense

- **Present tense** verbs tell about actions that happen now.
- Add **-s** to most verbs to tell what one person or thing does now.

    Greg **sings**.

Look at the picture. Write **-s** at the end of the verbs that show the actions of one person or thing.

1. Greg make _____ a mask.

2. Tam clip _____ the mask.

3. Greg help _____ Tam.

4. Tam twist _____ the mask.

5. Greg put _____ it on.

EXTENSION: Have the children read the sentences after they write -s at the end of the verbs. Then have them draw a circle around the verbs that tell what each person is doing now.

Book 1.3
Greg's Mask

5

McGraw-Hill School Division

Present Tense

- The **tense** of a verb tells when the action takes place.
- Some verbs tell about action that happens now.
- These verbs are in the **present tense**.
- Add **-s** to most verbs to tell what one person or thing does now.

    Tam **snips** the mask.

Choose a verb from the box. Write the correct verb in the sentence.

flips	makes	blinks	likes	sings

1. Bat _____.

2. Owl _____.

3. Greg _____ a mask.

4. Tam _____ Greg's mask.

5. Bird _____.

Book 1.3
Greg's Mask

EXTENSION: Have the children think of words that tell their actions when they are making an art project. Make a list of these words on a chart, putting **-s** at the end of each if appropriate.

Capital Letters in Book Titles

- The important words in a book title begin with a capital letter.
- Draw a line under the title of a book.

  <u>Little Red Riding Hood</u>

Read the titles. Write them correctly on the lines.

1. Goldilocks and the three bears

_____

- - - - - - - - - - - - - - - - -

_____

2. Three Billy goats gruff

_____

- - - - - - - - - - - - - - - - -

Read the sentences. Draw a line under the title of a book. Capitalize the important words in the title.

3. Tam reads cinderella.

4. Greg likes to read masks you can make.

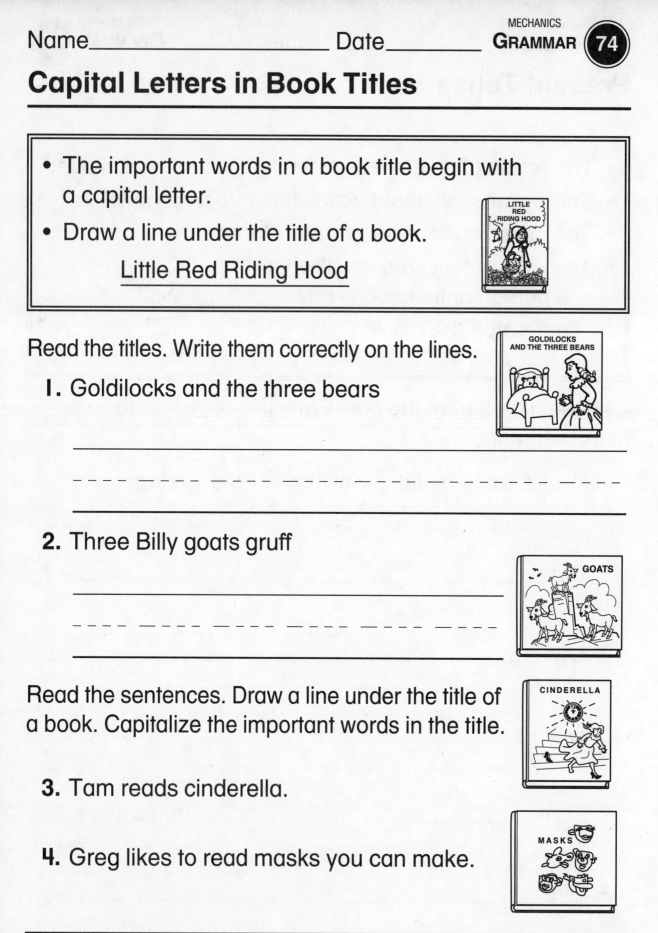

EXTENSION: Have the children look at books in the class library or school library. They should locate the titles and the capital letters in the titles.

Book 1.3
Greg's Mask
4

McGraw-Hill School Division

Present Tense

Mark the letter next to the verb that makes each sentence tell about the present.

I. Greg's class _____ masks.

Ⓐ make   Ⓑ makes   Ⓒ snap

2. Tam _____ it here.

Ⓐ snips   Ⓑ made   Ⓒ snap

3. Tam _____ it here.

Ⓐ twist   Ⓑ twisted   Ⓒ twists

4. Miss Wills _____ the new mask.

Ⓐ likes   Ⓑ like   Ⓒ liked

5. Greg _____ Tam the mask.

Ⓐ show   Ⓑ shows   Ⓒ showed

Present Tense

> - The **tense** of a verb tells when the action takes place.
> - Some verbs tell about action that happens now.
> - These verbs are in the **present tense**.
> - Add **-s** to most verbs to tell what one person or thing does now.

Write the sentences. Add **-s** to the verbs.

1. Greg sing.

_____

- -

_____

2. Tam clip it.

_____

- -

_____

3. Miss Wills like my mask.

_____

_____

4. Greg put on his mask.

_____

- -

_____

5. Tam make a new mask.

_____

- -

_____

McGraw-Hill School Division

Past Tense

- Some verbs tell about actions that already happened.
- These verbs are in the **past tense**.
- Most verbs in the past tense end in *-ed*.

   The owls **watched** the sun.

Read the sentences. Circle the verbs that tell about actions that already happened.

1. The owls watched the sun.

2. The owls looked at Sam.

3. Sam talked to Mom and Pop.

4. Chuck asked the owls about the sun.

5. A star winked at Sam.

McGraw-Hill School Division

EXTENSION: Have the children think of actions they took earlier today. Then have them tell sentences about those actions.

Past Tense

> - Some verbs tell about actions in the past.
> - Most verbs in the past end with **-ed**.
>   Mom **talked** to Sam.

Read the sentences. Circle the verb that tells about past actions.

1. We ___watch, watched___ the owls.

2. Sam ___want, wanted___ to sing.

3. The star ___wink, winked___ at Sam.

4. The mouse ___crunch, crunched___ .

5. Mom and Pop ___look, looked___ at Sam.

McGraw-Hill School Division

EXTENSION: The children can draw pictures to illustrate one of the sentences they completed above.

Writing Past Tense Verbs

- Some verbs tell about actions that already happened.
- These verbs are in the past tense.
- Most verbs in the past tense end in **-ed**.

    The frog **jumped**.

Write a past tense verb that tells about the picture.
Find the verb in the box.

looked	hiked	wanted	liked	winked

1. Mom and Pop _____ .

2. Chuck _____ at Baby Owl.

3. A star _____ at Sam.

4. Mom _____ Sam to sing whoo.

5. Sam _____ to sing a little song.

EXTENSION: Have the children write a past tense verb for their favorite activity. Then have them write a sentence using the word.

McGraw-Hill School Division

Names with Capital Letters

> • The special name of a person or place begins
>   with a capital letter.
>
>   **Jean** lives in **New York**.

Write the sentences.

Begin each person's name with a capital letter.

Begin each place name with a capital letter.

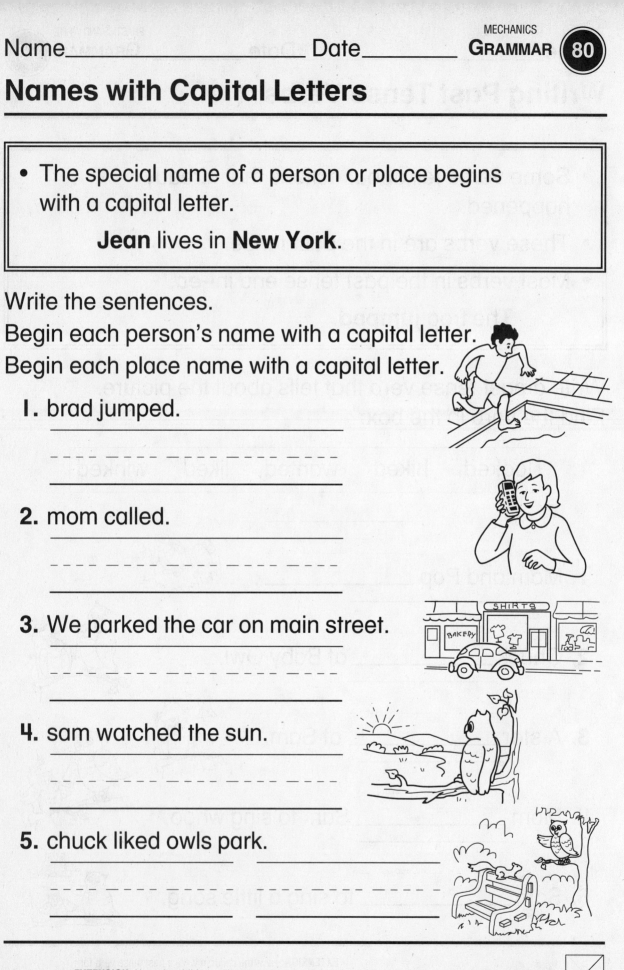

I. brad jumped.

_____

_ _ _ _ _ _ _ _ _ _ _ _ _ _ _ _ _

_____

2. mom called.

_____

_ _ _ _ _ _ _ _ _ _ _ _ _ _ _ _ _

_____

3. We parked the car on main street.

_____

_ _ _ _ _ _ _ _ _ _ _ _ _ _ _ _ _

_____

4. sam watched the sun.

_____

_ _ _ _ _ _ _ _ _ _ _ _ _ _ _ _ _

_____

5. chuck liked owls park.

_____   _____

_ _ _ _ _ _ _ _ _ _   _ _ _ _ _ _ _ _ _ _

_____   _____

McGraw-Hill School Division

EXTENSION: Have the children write proper names and
place names with capital letters.

Book 1.3
Sam's Song

5

Past Tense

Read each sentence. Look at the verb in ( ). Write
the verb in past tense to complete the sentence.

1. Mom _____ Sam. (watch)

2. The owls _____ food. (want)

3. Pam _____ at Max. (look)

4. I _____ on a star. (wish)

5. Pop _____ up. (jump)

More Practice with Past Tense

- Some verbs tell about actions that already happened.
- These verbs are in the **past tense**.
- Most verbs in the past tense end in *-ed*.

Circle the past tense verbs.

1. Mom and Pop watched Sam.

2. They wanted Sam to eat.

3. Sam liked to sing.

4. Mom, Pop, and Chuck sang.

5. Sam wished on a star.

Is and *Are*

- The words *is* and *are* are verbs that tell about the present.

    The snake <u>is</u> on the log.

    The big snakes <u>are</u> on the log.

Read the sentences. Draw a circle around the verbs *is* and *are*.

1. The big snakes are together.

2. The baby snakes are in shells.

3. That baby snake is out of the shell.

4. The snakes are safe.

5. A snake is safe in a log.

Book 1.3
Snakes

EXTENSION: Have the children tell sentences that have *is* or *are* as verbs.

83

Is and *Are*

- The words *is* and *are* are verbs that tell about the present.
- The word *is* tells about one person, place, or thing.
- The word *are* tells about more than one person, place, or thing.

The snake **is** hungry.　　The snakes **are** hungry.

One snake 　　More than one snake

Read these sentences. Find *is* in a sentence and draw one snake. Find *are* in a sentence and draw more than one snake.

1. That snake is on the rock.

2. The snakes are big.

3. The snakes are safe under the rocks.

4. That snake is not my pet.

5. The baby snake is out of the shell.

EXTENSION: Have the children find the word in each
sentence that tells them to write *is* or *are*.

Book 1.3
Snakes 5

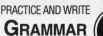

Is and *Are*

- The words *is* and *are* are verbs that tell about the present.

- The word *is* tells about one person, place, or thing.

- The word *are* tells about more than one person, place, or thing.

    This **is** a safe snake.

    These snakes **are** not safe.

Read the sentences.

Write *is* in the sentences that tell about one person, place, or thing.

Write *are* in the sentences that tell about more than one person, place, or thing.

1. There _____ a lot of snakes in the world.

2. The snakes _____ moving.

3. A snake's skin _____ made of scales.

4. The snake _____ safe in a log.

5. This snake _____ not safe.

Book 1.3
Snakes

EXTENSION: Have the children draw pictures and *is* on the pictures of one and *are* on those that are more than one.

Correcting Sentences with *Is* and *Are*

> • Begin every sentence with a capital letter.
>
> • End a statement with a period.
>
> • End an exclamation with an exclamation point.

Read the sentences. Circle the words that need to be capitalized. Write the correct end mark.

1. the snake is in a log

2. is a snake in the tree

3. look at all those snakes

4. are they safe snakes

5. that snake is in a hot land

6. where are all the snakes

7. look out for the big snake

8. that snake is not my pet

EXTENSION: Have the children make the incorrect
sentences correct.

Book 1.3
Snakes

8

McGraw-Hill School Division

Test

Read each sentence. Circle the correct verb.

1. There _____ a lot of snakes.

    are   is

2. There _____ big snakes and small snakes.

    are   is

3. One snake _____ in the log.

    are   is

4. One snake _____ in the damp land.

    are   is

5. That _____ a big rat!

    are   is

More Practice With *Is* And *Are*

> - The verbs *is* and *are* tell about the present.
> - The verb *is* tells about one person, place, or thing.
> - The verb *are* tells about more than one person, place, or thing.

Read each sentence aloud. Write *is* and *are* where they belong.

I. Most snakes _____ safe.

2. But one snake _____ not safe.

3. One snake _____ on the log.

4. Some snakes _____ making their mouths big.

5. Where _____ a snake safe?

McGraw-Hill School Division

Contractions with *Not*

> - A **contraction** is a short form of two words.
>
>   You <u>are not</u> going on a hike. — Long form
>
>   You <u>aren't</u> going on a hike.   — Short form

Read the sentences. Draw a circle around the short form of two words.

1. Greg isn't packing for a trip.

2. They aren't packing for a trip.

3. You aren't a singer.

4. You are not a singer.

5. Pam is not getting her pack.

6. Pam isn't getting her pack.

6 Book 1.3
Let's Camp Out!

EXTENSION: Have the children think of sentences with contractions. Write the contractions on a chart.

89

Contractions with *Not*

- A **contraction** is a short form of two words.
- An **apostrophe** (') takes the place of the letters that are left out.

> She is not picking up sticks. — is not
>
> She isn't picking up sticks. — isn't

Read the sentences. Draw a circle around the two words that were joined in the contractions.

1. Pam isn't looking at the Big Dipper.

   is not   not at   Pam is

2. Max isn't a singer.

   is not   Max is   not a

3. They aren't packing.

   are not   They are   not packing

4. Greg isn't picking up sticks.

   Greg is   is not   not picking

5. They aren't warmed up.

   are not   They are   not warmed

EXTENSION: Have the children look for contractions in trade books that have been read to them. Write the contractions they find on a chart.

90

Book 1.3
Let's Camp Out! 5

McGraw-Hill School Division

Contractions with *Not*

- A **contraction** is a short form of two words.

- An **apostrophe** (') takes the place of the letters that are left out.

Write the contraction for the underlined words in each sentence.

1. Cory <u>is not</u> picking up twigs.

_____

_ _ _ _ _ _ _ _ _ _ _ _ _

_____

2. She <u>is not</u> seeing the Big Dipper.

_____

_ _ _ _ _ _ _ _ _ _ _ _ _

_____

3. They <u>are not</u> finding the food.

_____

_ _ _ _ _ _ _ _ _ _ _ _ _

_____

4. They <u>are not</u> hiking.

_____

_ _ _ _ _ _ _ _ _ _ _ _ _

_____

5. She <u>is not</u> hiking.

_____

_ _ _ _ _ _ _ _ _ _ _ _ _

_____

5 Book 1.3
Let's Camp Out!

EXTENSION: Have the children rewrite the sentences in the long form with both words.

91

Contractions with *Not*

- A **contraction** is a short form of two words.
- A **contraction** is a way of saying two words as one.
- Two words are joined and a letter is left out.
- An **apostrophe** (') takes the place of the letters that are left out.

You **are not** going on a hike.
You **aren't** going on a hike.

Correct the contractions. Put in the apostrophe (').
Write the contraction.

1. That isnt our food. _____

2. They arent making a fire. _____

3. Greg isnt finding our tent. _____

4. Isnt that a big tent? _____

5. They arent sleeping. _____

EXTENSION: Have the children tell the two words that were joined to make the contractions in this exercise.

Book 1.3
Let's Camp Out!

/5

McGraw-Hill School Division

Contractions with *Not*

Circle the two words that make the contraction.

1. Greg isn't going on a trip.

Greg is not going on a trip.

2. Greg isn't going to get a pack.

Greg is not going to get a pack.

3. They aren't making a fire.

They are not making a fire.

4. They aren't sleeping in a tent.

They are not sleeping in a tent.

5. Greg isn't looking for the Big Dipper.

Greg is not looking for the Big Dipper.

6. They aren't sleeping in a tent.

They are not sleeping in a tent.

Contractions with *Not*

> - A **contraction** is a short form of two words.
> - An **apostrophe** (') takes the place of the letters that are left out.

Look at the picture above. Read the sentences about it. Circle the contractions you find.

1. You aren't going to sleep in a tent.

2. Meg isn't going to camp.

3. Isn't that good food?

4. They aren't going to put up a tent.

5. They think that camping isn't fun.

6. Greg isn't lighting the fire.

7. Aren't the children going to sing?

8. They aren't going on a hike.

McGraw-Hill School Division

Verbs

Read the sentences in the box. Look at the part with the line under it. What is the best way to say this part? Mark the letter for your answer.

> Frog jumps. <u>Jumping Stan.</u> The others jump.
>   (1)

I. Ⓐ Stan jumps.
   Ⓑ Stan jumping.
   Ⓒ Stan jump.

> Mom, Pop, and Chuck sing. <u>Sam with them.</u>
>   (2)

2. Ⓐ Sam with Chuck sing.
   Ⓑ Pop and Sam sings.
   Ⓒ Sam sings with them.

> <u>Owl blink.</u> Stan watches Owl. Stan blinks like Owl.
>   (3)

3. Ⓐ Owl blinks.
   Ⓑ Blink Owl.
   Ⓒ Owl blinking.

> Last night, I wanted to eat. <u>I look for pizza.</u>
>   (4)

4. Ⓐ I looks for Pizza
   Ⓑ I looked for pizza.
   Ⓒ Pizza for I look.

Go on

There are a lot of snakes. <u>One snake are on the log.</u> It is a big
snake.   (5)

5. Ⓐ One snake is on the log.
Ⓑ One snakes are on the log.
Ⓒ Snakes is on the log.

The stars are bright. Where are they? <u>The stars is in the sky.</u>
                                           (6)

6. Ⓐ Stars in the sky.
Ⓑ The star are in the sky.
Ⓒ The stars are in the sky.

<u>Bat aren't in the tree.</u> Find Bat. Bat is inside the barn.
     (7)

7. Ⓐ Bat are not in the tree.
Ⓑ Bat isn't in the tree.
Ⓒ Bat are in the tree.

<u>Greg and Tam isn't in school.</u> Greg is at home. Tam isn't in
school.   (8)

8. Ⓐ Greg and Tam is in school.
Ⓑ Greg and Tam are in school.
Ⓒ Greg and Tam aren't in school.

Was and *Were*

> • The words *was* and *were* are verbs that tell about the past.
>
> • The word *was* tells about one person, place, or thing.
>
>   Mike **was** in his Dad's store.

Read the sentences. Write *was* in each sentence.

_____

1. Dad _____ happy.

2. Mike _____ in the store.

3. No one _____ home.

4. Miss Lin_____with Mike.

5. The store_____full of people.

5 Book 1.4
The Shopping List

EXTENSION: Ask students to use the words *was* and *were*
to write sentences about what they did yesterday.

97

Was and *Were*

- The words *was* and *were* are verbs that tell about the past.
- The word *was* tells about one person, place, or thing.
- The word *were* tells about more than one person, place, or thing.

  Gran and Ann **were** in the store.

Read the sentence about each picture.
Circle the verb for more than one person, place, or thing.

1. Mom and Dad were happy.

2. The jam and rice were for supper.

3. Mike and Dad were smiling.

4. The five plums were in a bag.

5. Grapes were on the list.

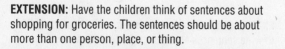

EXTENSION: Have the children think of sentences about shopping for groceries. The sentences should be about more than one person, place, or thing.

Book 1.4
The Shopping List

5

McGraw-Hill School Division

Was and *Were*

- The words *was* and *were* are verbs that tell about the past.
- The word *was* tells about one person, place, or thing.

  Mike **was** smiling.

- The word *were* tells about more than one person, place, or thing.

  Fran and Ann **were** smiling.

Read the sentences. Write *was* for one person, place, or thing. Write *were* for more than one person, place, or thing.

1. Mike _____ in the store.

2. Fran _____ in the store.

3. Fran and Ann _____ there.

4. Tin cans and glass jars _____ on the shelves.

5. Fran and Ann _____ trying to help.

---

5 Book 1.4
The Shopping List

EXTENSION: Have the children change the sentences with one person, place, or thing to sentences with more than one.

99

Capital Letters

> • The name of each day begins with a capital letter.
> • The name of each month begins with a capital letter.
> • The name of a holiday begins with a capital letter.

Read the sentences. Circle each word that should begin with a capital letter.

1. Ann Gomez was home on thursday.

2. Last april was Mike's birthday.

3. Ann and Fran were at the thanksgiving dinner.

4. Miss Lin was celebrating new year's day.

5. Mike was looking for birthday presents on sunday.

6. It was cold last november.

EXTENSION: Have the students write sentences that use names of days, months, and holidays.

McGraw-Hill School Division

Was and *Were*

Circle and write *was* or *were* to complete each sentence.

_____

\- \- \- \- \- \- \- \- \- \- \- \- \- \- \- \- \- \-

1. Mike _____ glad to see Mom.

was   were

_____

\- \- \- \- \- \- \- \- \- \- \- \- \- \- \- \- \-

2. Miss Lin and Dad _____ helping.

was   were

_____

\- \- \- \- \- \- \- \- \- \- \- \- \- \- \- \- \-

3. Ann and Fran _____ helping.

was   were

_____

\- \- \- \- \- \- \- \- \- \- \- \- \- \- \- \- \-

4. There _____ something else to get.

was   were

_____

\- \- \- \- \- \- \- \- \- \- \- \- \- \- \- \- \-

5. It _____ not milk.

was   were

More Practice with *Was* and *Were*

- The words *was* and *were* are verbs that tell about the past.
- The word *was* tells about one person, place, or thing.
- The word *were* tells about more than one person, place, or thing.

Read each sentence. Write *was* or *were* in the blank.
Color the pictures. The sentences tell you how.

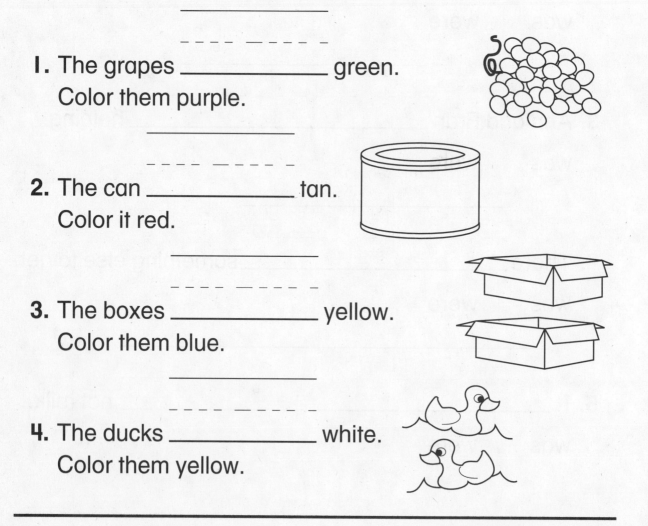

1. The grapes _____ green.
   Color them purple.

2. The can _____ tan.
   Color it red.

3. The boxes _____ yellow.
   Color them blue.

4. The ducks _____ white.
   Color them yellow.

Book 1.4
The Shopping List / 4

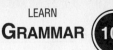
Has and *Have*

* The words *has* and *have* are verbs that tell about the present.

* The word *has* tells about one person, place, or thing.

  Yasmin has the best ducks.

  Yasmin is one person.

  The verb is *has*.

Circle the verb for one person, place, or thing in each sentence.

1. Tim has pictures of fish.

2. Kate has trucks.

3. One truck has four wheels.

4. The duck has feathers.

5. The lake has ducks.

Book 1.4
Yasmin's Ducks

EXTENSION: Have children make up sentences with one person, place, or thing, and *has* as the verb.

Has and *Have*

- The words *has* and *have* are verbs that tell about the present.
- The word *have* tells about more than one person, place, or thing.

Circle the verb that tells about more than one person, place, or thing.

1. The ducks have fun in the lake.

2. The child has ducks.

3. The children have many ducks.

4. Yasmin and Mack have water and oil.

5. The ducks have food.

6. The children have a good time.

7. The ducks have a home.

8. Yasmin has many ducks.

EXTENSION: Ask students to look around the classroom. Have them use the words *has* and *have* to write sentences about what they see.

Book 1.4
Yasmin's Ducks

8

McGraw-Hill School Division

Has and Have

> • The words *has* and *have* are verbs that tell about the past.
>
> • The word *has* tells about one person, place, or thing.
>
> • The word *have* tells about more than one person, place, or thing.

Read each sentence. Then write *has* for one person, place, or thing. Write *have* for sentences with more than one person, place, or thing.

1. This duck _____ fun with the children.

2. The duck _____ plenty of food.

3. Yasmin _____ a book about ducks.

4. Ducks _____ oil on their feathers.

5. Yasmin and Tim _____ ducks.

Correcting Sentences with *Has* and *Have*

- Begin every sentence with a capital letter.
- End every sentence with a period.
- End every question with a question mark.

Write each sentence correctly.

1. the children have show and tell

_____

_____

2. Does Tim have pictures of fish

_____

_____

3. mom has ducks too

_____

_____

4. Kate has a picture of fire trucks

_____

_____

5. do Kate and Mack have pictures for show and tell

_____

_____

EXTENSION: Have children write additional statements and questions without end marks. Then have them exchange sentences and put in the end marks.

Book 1.4
Yasmin's Ducks

5

McGraw-Hill School Division

Test

Read each sentence. Circle the correct verb for each sentence.

1. Yasmin _____ a duck.

   has   have   do

2. Ducks _____ oil next to their tails.

   has   have   are

3. The duck _____ a friend.

   has   have   are

4. That duck _____ food.

   can   has   have

5. The ducks _____ fun.

   do   has   have

McGraw-Hill School Division

More Practice with *Has* and *Have*

- The words *has* and *have* are verbs that tell about the present.
- The word *has* tells about one person, place, or thing.
- The word *have* tells about more than one person, place, or thing.

Read each sentence aloud. Write the sentences to make them correct.

1. Yasmin have three ducks.

_____

_ _

_____

2. Yasmin's ducks has fun.

_____

_ _

_____

3. Pets has fun with us.

_____

_ _

_____

4. Mack have a pup.

_ _

_____

5. Ducks has a home.

_____

_ _

_____

Go and *Do*

- The verb *go* has a special form to tell about the past.
- Use *go* or *goes* to tell about something that happens in the present.

  Max **goes** out every day.

- Use *went* to tell about something that happened in the past.

  Max **went** out last night.

Read the sentences. Look for *go*, *goes*, and *went*.
Circle Present or Past.

I. We <u>go</u> to the country.

Present   Past

2. Max Mule <u>goes</u> to help Sam.

Present   Past

3. Sam <u>went</u> to Bob Bull for help.

Present   Past

4. Sam <u>went</u> to Kate Owl for help.

Present   Past

5. Sam <u>goes</u> to the lake.

Present   Past

EXTENSION: Have the children reread stories in their
reader to find *go*, *goes*, and *went*.

Go and Do

> - The verb *do* has a special form to tell about the past.
>
> - Use *do* or *does* to tell about something that happens in the present.
>
>   **Do** you like to clean corn cobs?
>
>   Sam **does** not have to be bigger.
>
> - Use *did* to tell about something that happened in the past.
>
>   Max Mule **did** help Sam.

Read the sentences. Circle the verbs that tell about the past.

1. Do bugs carry rope?

2. Why did Sam chomp on ten corn cobs?

3. Does running ten miles help Sam?

4. Sam did not grow one inch.

5. But Sam did not give up.

EXTENSION: The children can change the present verb tense sentences to past verb tense.

Book 1.4
The Knee-High Man 5

McGraw-Hill School Division

Go and *Do*

- The verb *go* has a special form to tell about the past.
- Use *went* to tell about something that happened in the past.

      Sam *went* to see Bob the Bull.

- The verb *do* has a special form to tell about the past.
- Use *did* to tell about something that happened in the past.

      Why *did* Sam want to be big?

Read the sentences. Write the verbs that tell about the past.

1. How _____ Kate Owl help Sam?   (do did)

2. Who _____ Sam have to fight?   (do did)

3. He _____ to see Kate Owl.   (go went)

4. Why _____ Sam want to be big?   (do did)

5. Sam _____ up a tree to look.   (go went)

---

5 Book 1.4
The Knee-High Man

EXTENSION: The children can compose sentences about
something that happened in the past.

111

Names with Capital Letters

> • The name of a person or place begins with a capital letter.
>
>   <u>M</u>ax <u>M</u>ule is big.

Circle the words that should begin with capital letters.

1. Sam went to see max mule.

2. Max did not help sam grow big.

3. Sam went to talk to bob bull.

4. Sam did what bob told him.

5. Sam went to new york.

EXTENSION: Have children write the above sentences correctly.

Book 1.4
The Knee-High Man

 5

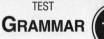

Test

Draw a line under each verb that tells about the present. Circle each verb that tells about the past.

1. Sam went up the tree.

2. Sam does not get help.

3. Kate and Owl did help.

4. Kate and Owl do the work.

5. Sam goes to the tree.

6. Sam went to get help.

7. Why do you go there?

8. Why did Sam go up a tree?

9. Sam goes to see Bob the Bull.

10. Sam went to see Bob the Bull.

More Practice with *Go* and *Do*

> • Use *go* or *goes* to tell about the present.
> • Use *went* to tell about the past.
> • Use *do* or *does* to tell about the present.
> • Use *did* to tell about the past.

Look at Picture 1. Read the sentences next to it.
Circle the sentences about the past.

1. Sam went to get help.

2. Sam does things to get big.

3. Sam did not want to fight.

4. Sam went to Kate the Owl.

Read the sentences next to Picture 2. Circle the
sentences that tell about the present.

5. Sam went for help.

6. Bob did not help.

7. He does not have to go out.

8. Sam does not fight.

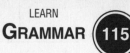
See and *Say*

> • The verb *see* has a special form to tell about the past.
> • Use *see* or *sees* to tell about the present.
>   Johnny Appleseed **sees** pink buds.
> • Use *saw* to tell about the past.
>   He **saw** people going west.

Write the underlined verb so that it tells about the past.

1. Johnny <u>sees</u> the trees. _____

2. He <u>sees</u> the people. _____

3. They <u>see</u> his smile. _____

4. Johnny <u>sees</u> the buds. _____

5. Then he <u>sees</u> apples. _____

See and *Say*

> - The verb *say* has a special form to tell about the past.
> - Use *say* and *says* to tell about the present.
> - Use *said* to tell about something that happened in the past.
>
>   I **say** something.   He **said** something.

Write the underlined verb so that it tells about the past.

1. Johnny <u>says</u> the ham was good. _____

2. He <u>says</u> he would rest. _____

3. He <u>says</u> the sun was up. _____

4. He <u>says</u>, "I'm Johnny." _____

5. They <u>say</u>, "Hello, Johnny." _____

McGraw-Hill School Division

See and *Say*

> • Use *see* or *sees* to tell about the present.
>
> > We **see** pink flowers.
>
> • Use *saw* to tell about something that happened in the past.
>
> > We **saw** pink buds.

Circle the word that makes each sentence tell about the past.

1. Johnny (saw, see, sees) a wolf in a trap.

2. One day, he (saw, see, sees) an old horse.

3. People (saw, see, sees) his pets.

Circle the word that makes each sentence tell about the present.

4. Johnny (saw, see, sees) many plants.

5. He could (saw, see, sees) rain.

6. He (saw, see, sees) many people.

Book 1.4
Johnny Appleseed

EXTENSION: Have the children write present or past tense sentences about seeing apples.

Commas in a Letter

> - Use a comma between the day and year in a date.
> - Use a comma between the name of a city and a state.
> - Use a comma after the greeting in a letter.
> - Use a comma after the closing in a letter.

Read the sentences. Put commas where they belong.

Dear Sally

    I saw Johnny Appleseed in Ohio.
He planted many apples.

        Your friend
        Meg

July 4 1803

Dear Meg

    I wish Johnny would come to Springfield Illinois.
     He can see how our apples are growing.

        Your friend
        Sally

EXTENSION: Have the children write letters about Johnny Appleseed.

McGraw-Hill School Division

Book 1.4
Johnny Appleseed 5

Test

Draw a line under the verb that tells about the present. Circle the verb that tells about the past.

1. Johnny Appleseed saw apple trees.

2. Johnny Appleseed sees apple trees.

3. Johnny said, "Plant apple seeds."

4. Johnny says, "Plant apple seeds."

5. Johnny sees people planting trees.

6. Johnny saw people planting trees.

7. Johnny said he liked animals.

8. He says he likes animals.

9. The people said they liked Johnny.

10. The people say they like Johnny.

More Practice with *See* and *Say*

> - Use *see* or *sees* to tell about the present.
> - Use *saw* to tell about the past.
> - Use *say* or *says* to tell about the present.
> - Use *said* to tell about the past.

Read each sentence aloud.
Circle the sentences that tell
about the past. Underline the
sentences that tell about
the present.

1. Johnny sees rain and fog.

2. Johnny says he wants a place to rest.

3. Johnny said, "Plant my apple seeds in Springfield,
   Illinois."

4. Johnny saw many places for apple trees.

5. Johnny sees many smiles in Mansfield, Ohio.

6. He says he likes trees.

7. People saw Johnny.

8. They said hello.

McGraw-Hill School Division

More Contractions with *Not*

- A **contraction** is a short form of two words.
- A **contraction** is a short way of saying two words.
- An **apostrophe** (') takes the place of the letters that are left out.

was not	wasn't
were not	weren't

Read the sentences. Circle the short form of two words.

1. The house wasn't on fire.

2. They weren't going to a fire.

3. They weren't in the truck.

4. There wasn't any work to do.

5. He wasn't putting out a fire.

6. They weren't going down the pole.

7. The pole wasn't tall.

8. The trucks weren't blue.

Book 1.4
Ring! Ring! Ring! Put Out the Fire!!

121

More Contractions with *Not*

- A **contraction** is a short form of two words.
- An **apostrophe** (') takes the place of the letters that are left out.

    do not   don't

Read the sentences. Find the short form of two words. Draw a circle around the contraction.

1. Didn't you see the fire truck?

2. The fire truck didn't stop.

3. I don't see the fire.

4. They didn't need to work.

5. We don't have a fire here.

EXTENSION: Have the children tell which two words are joined in the contractions on this page.

Book 1.4
Ring! Ring! Ring! Put Out the Fire!!

5

McGraw-Hill School Division

More Contractions with *Not*

> • A **contraction** is a short form of two words.
> • An **apostrophe** (') takes the place of the letters that are left out.
>
> | | |
> |---|---|
> | was not | wasn't |
> | were not | weren't |
> | do not | don't |
> | did not | didn't |

Read the sentences. Circle the two words that make the contraction in each sentence.

1. The firefighters don't always need masks.

do not   was not   did not

2. The firefighters weren't on their way.

were not   was not   do not

3. They didn't rush away.

did not   was not   do not

4. They didn't go down the pole.

did not   was not   do not

5. That wasn't the ladder.

was not   did not   do not

McGraw-Hill School Division

5

Book 1.4
Ring! Ring! Ring! Put Out the Fire!!

EXTENSION: The children can think of sentences about fire prevention that include these contractions.

123

More Contractions with *Not*

> • A **contraction** is a short form of two words.
> • Use an **apostrophe** (') in place of <u>o</u> in a contraction with <u>not</u>.
>
>   was not   wasn't

On the lines, write the contractions for the words in ( ).

_____

1. (Do not)_____stop, the firefighters are on the way.

_____

2. (Does not) _____ the fireman work fast?

_____

3. The fireman (was not) _____ in the fire truck.

_____

4. They (were not) _____ in the fire truck.

_____

5. The firefighters (were not) _____ working.

EXTENSION: The children can identify the two words that are put together to make each contraction.

Book 1.4
Ring! Ring! Ring! Put Out the Fire!!

McGraw-Hill School Division

5

Test

Write the contraction for the underlined words.

1. The house <u>was not</u> on fire.

_____

- -

_____

2. The men <u>did not</u> rush.

_____

- -

_____

3. <u>Do not</u> go near the fire.

_____

- -

_____

4. They <u>were not</u> at home.

_____

- -

_____

5. She <u>did not</u> see the truck.

_____

- -

_____

More Practice With Contractions

- A **contraction** is a short form of two words.

- An **apostrophe** (') takes the place of the letters that are left out.

Look at the picture. Read the sentences about it. Circle the contraction for the underlined words.

1. They <u>were not</u> going down the pole.

    weren't   don't   wasn't

2. They <u>do not</u> like smoke.

    weren't   don't   didn't

3. They <u>did not</u> need masks.

    didn't   don't   weren't

4. One <u>was not</u> ready.

    wasn't   didn't   weren't

5. They <u>were not</u> going to a fire.

    wasn't   weren't   didn't

McGraw-Hill School Division

Book 1.4
Ring! Ring! Ring! Put Out the Fire!!

5

More About Verbs

Read the sentences in the box. Look at the part with the line under it. Is there a mistake? How do you make it right? Mark your answer.

Five plums were in a bag. <u>A jar of jam were on the shelf.</u> (1)

1. **Ⓐ** Take away *were*.
   Ⓑ Change *were* to *was*.
   Ⓒ Do not change.

The child has ducks. <u>The children has many ducks.</u> (2)

2. **Ⓐ** Change *has* to *have*.
   Ⓑ Take away *has*.
   Ⓒ Do not change.

<u>Yasmin have many ducks.</u> The ducks have a home. (3)

3. **Ⓐ** Take away *have*.
   Ⓑ Change *have* to *has*.
   Ⓒ Do not change.

Sam went to get help. <u>Sam go up the tree.</u> (4)

4. **Ⓐ** Change *go* to *went*.
   Ⓑ Take away *go*.
   Ⓒ Do not change.

Go on ➡

More About Verbs

> Sam went to see Bob the Bull. <u>Where do Sam go?</u>
> (5)

5. Ⓐ Change *do* to *did*.
   Ⓑ Change *go* to *went*.
   Ⓒ Do not change.

> <u>Long ago, Johnny says he liked apples.</u> He planted apple trees. (6)

6. Ⓐ Take away *says*.
   Ⓑ Change *says* to *said*.
   Ⓒ Do not change.

> People saw apple trees. <u>Johnny see people smile.</u>
> (7)

7. Ⓐ Change *see* to *saw*.
   Ⓑ Take away *see*.
   Ⓒ Do not change.

> <u>We do'nt like smoke.</u> We aren't going to the fire.
> (8)

8. Ⓐ Change *do'nt* to *don't*.
   Ⓑ Change *do'nt* to *doesn't*.
   Ⓒ Do not change.

Adjectives

> • An **adjective** is a word that tells about a person, place, or thing.
>
> • Some adjectives tell how people, places, or things look or sound.
>
> a <u>tall</u> man   a <u>big</u> house   a <u>loud</u> sound

Read the sentences. Draw a circle around the adjective in each sentence.

I. One bright morning, Pig went to the pond.

2. That is a nice pond.

3. There is a little mouse in the pond.

4. The silly animals jumped.

5. The wet pig got out.

 Book 1.5/Unit 1
Seven Sillies

EXTENSION: Have the children make up sentences that
tell how things look or sound.

129

Adjectives in Sentences

> • Some **adjectives** tell how things taste, smell, or feel.
>
> This is <u>sour</u> food.
>
> That flower has a <u>sweet</u> smell.
>
> The kitten has <u>soft</u> fur.

Read the sentences. Find the words that tell about how things taste, smell, or feel. Draw a circle around each adjective.

1. We ate a tasty meal.

2. The bed is soft.

3. This rock is hard.

4. The dog has wet hair.

5. What is that sweet smell?

Book 1.5/Unit 1
Seven Sillies

5

Writing Adjectives in Sentences

- An **adjective** is a word that tells about a person, place, or thing.
- Some adjectives tell how people, places, or things look or sound.
- Some adjectives tell how things taste, smell, or feel.

Read the adjectives in the box. Write an adjective in each sentence.

| big | hot | sweet | hard | loud |

1. Pig looked into the _____ pond.

2. I heard the baby's _____ cry.

3. The _____ candy tastes good.

4. The _____ rock fell in the pond.

5. The _____ sun shines on Pig.

Names with Capital Letters

> • The special name of a person or place begins with a capital letter.

Read the sentences. Circle the words that should begin with a capital letter.

1. Pig went to blue pond.

2. max heard tam's loud call.

3. sam bought fresh eggs from jet mart.

4. green street is near the big pond.

5. The silly animals looked for bird park.

6. The park is next to main street.

7. galleria mall is big.

8. It is in dallas.

EXTENSION: Have the children write sentences telling about the street where they live.

Book 1.5/Unit 1
Seven Sillies 8

McGraw-Hill School Division

Adjectives

Choose the adjective to complete the sentences.
Write the correct answer on the line.

1. The _____ pig is in the pond.

    pink   out   see

2. I like _____ food.

    was   be   hot

3. Max is a _____ cat.

    saw   fat   and

4. Pam ate a _____ cake.

    sweet   food   pond

5. Tam has a _____ hat.

    find   feel   blue

Name_____ Date_____

Adjectives

- An adjective is a word that tells about a person, place, or thing.
- Some adjectives tell how people, places, or things look and sound.
- Some adjectives tell how people, places, or things taste, smell, or feel.

Circle the adjective that tells about the picture. Then write the adjective on the line.

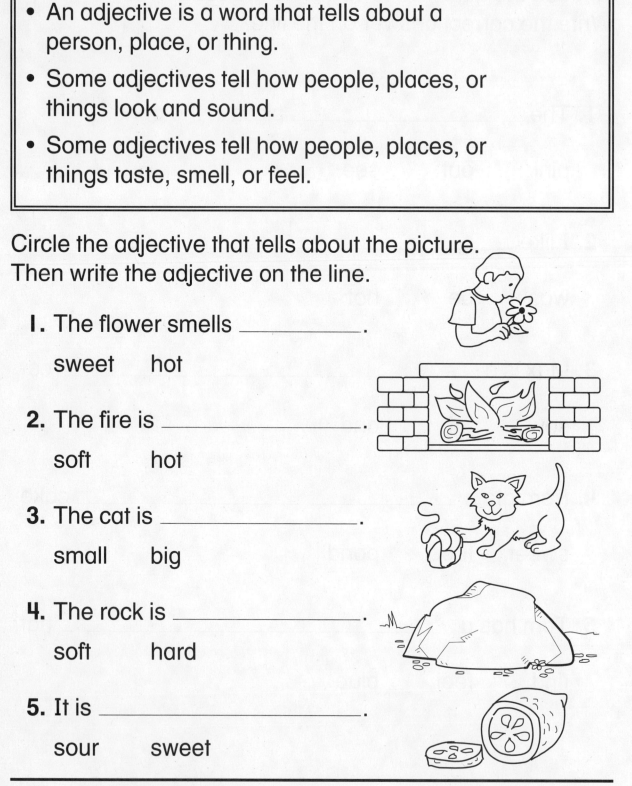

1. The flower smells _____.

   sweet   hot

2. The fire is _____.

   soft   hot

3. The cat is _____.

   small   big

4. The rock is _____.

   soft   hard

5. It is _____.

   sour   sweet

McGraw-Hill School Division

EXTENSION: The students can work in groups or pairs to think of sentences that have adjectives. Then have their partner or group tell whether the adjective tells about look, sound, taste, smell, or feel.

134

Book 1.5/Unit 1
Seven Sillies

 5

Adjectives That Compare

> • You can use adjectives to compare people, places, or things.
>
> • Add **-er** to an adjective to compare two people, places, or things.
>
> Mouse is smaller than Owl.

Circle the adjective that compares.

1. Pam is taller than Max.

2. Tam is older than Mouse.

3. Candy is sweeter than bread.

4. Beds are softer than rocks.

5. Owl is faster than Mouse.

6. Black is darker than white.

McGraw-Hill School Division

6 Book 1.5/Unit 1
Shrinking Mouse

EXTENSION: The children can think of sentences that compare their size with adults and siblings.

135

Adjectives That Compare

- You can use adjectives to compare people, places, or things.

- Add **-est** to compare three or more people, places, or things.

    Fox is the **biggest** animal in this story.

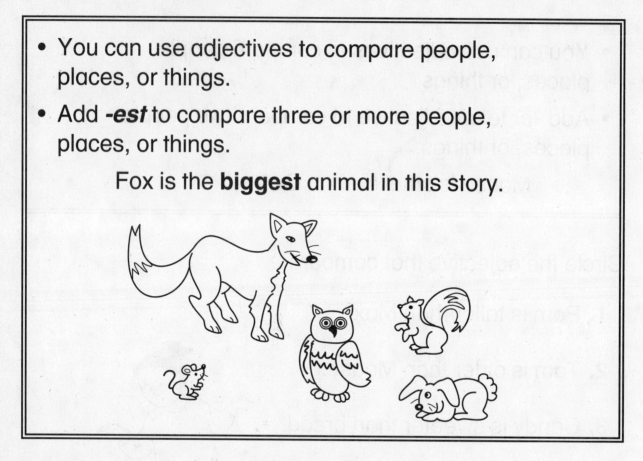

Read the sentences. Circle the adjective that ends in *est*.

1. Mouse is the smallest animal.

2. Rabbit hops the fastest of all.

3. Who is the biggest animal?

4. Who was the oldest animal?

5. That is the highest tree.

EXTENSION: Have children name something that is the biggest thing they have ever seen.

McGraw-Hill School Division

Writing Adjectives That Compare

- You can use adjectives to compare people, places, or things.
- Add **-er** to an adjective to compare two people, places, or things.
- Add **-est** to compare three or more people, places, or things.

Read the sentences. Write the word that compares.

1. The dog is _____ than Mouse.

  older   oldest

2. My arm is _____ than his.

  big   bigger

3. Who is the _____ person in class?

  smaller   smallest

4. He is the _____ boy in the school.

  taller   tallest

5. It is the _____ flower in the bunch.

  nicer   nicest

Book 1.5/Unit 1
Shrinking Mouse

EXTENSION: Have children tell what is being compared in each sentence.

Correcting Sentences

> • Begin every sentence with a capital letter.
> • End every sentence with a special mark.

Circle the letters that should be capitals.
Make the correct end mark for each sentence.

1. that is the biggest house

2. tim's hat is bigger than yours

3. how big is your coat

4. he is the smallest boy

5. that train is longer than the bus

McGraw-Hill School Division

EXTENSION: Have the children write sentences about
"Shrinking Mouse." Then exchange sentences to proofread
for capital letters and ending marks.

Book 1.5/Unit 1
Shrinking Mouse 5

Adjectives That Compare

Find the sentence that compares two or more things. Mark your answer.

1. Ⓐ Mouse is small.

    Ⓑ I like Mouse.

    Ⓒ Mouse is smaller than Owl.

2. Ⓐ Owl is the fastest bird.

    Ⓑ Owl is Mouse's friend.

    Ⓒ Owl is fast.

3. Ⓐ Who is the smallest boy?

    Ⓑ Who is small?

    Ⓒ Why are you here?

4. Ⓐ A rose is a sweet flower.

    Ⓑ A rose is sweeter than a pig.

    Ⓒ Who likes sweet things?

Adjectives That Compare

- Adjectives compare people, places, or things.
- Add **-er** to an adjective to compare two people, places, or things.
- Add **-est** to compare three or more people, places, or things.

Read each group of words aloud. Write the words in order. Write *2* for sentences comparing two. Write *3* for sentences comparing three or more.

I. Mouse is smaller than Owl. _____

2. Rabbit was the fastest of the animals. _____

3. Squirrel is smaller than Fox. _____

4. Mouse is the smallest of the three animals. _____

5. Tam is taller than Pam. _____

Color Words

> • Some **adjectives** tell about colors.
>
> blue   red   green

Read the sentences. Draw a circle around the color word in each sentence.

1. The red cake is sweet.

2. Pam has blue eyes.

3. Do you have green hair?

4. The rose is red.

5. The leaves are green.

Color Words

• Some adjectives tell about colors.

The sky is <u>black</u> at night.

Read the sentences. Draw a circle around the color word in each sentence.

1. Yellow flowers smell best.

2. I have a black dog.

3. My cat is white.

4. Have you seen black flowers?

5. I like red flowers.

McGraw-Hill School Division

EXTENSION: Have the children make up sentences with color words.

Book 1.5/Unit 1
You Can't Smell a Flower with Your Ear! 5

Writing Color Words in Sentences

> • Some adjectives tell about colors.
>
> | red | blue | brown | green |
> |-----|------|-------|-------|
> | yellow | white | pink | black |

Write a color word to complete the sentence.

1. I like _____ flowers.

2. My eyes are _____.

3. My friend has _____ eyes.

4. I have a _____ toy.

5. My shoes are _____.

EXTENSION: Have children make a list of their favorite colors.

Contractions

> • Use an apostrophe (') in place of **_o_** in a
> contraction with <u>not</u>.

Write each sentence on the line.
Put an apostrophe (') in each contraction.

I. Why arent you looking at the white flowers?

_____

2. Cant you smell the green grass?

_____

3. Doesnt your nose smell the red rose?

_____

4. Bob and Tim werent wearing orange coats.

_____

5. Tam wont taste the brown cake.

_____

EXTENSION: Have the children draw colored balloons and
write a contraction on each one.

Book 1.5/Unit 1
You Can't Smell a Flower with Your Ear! 5

McGraw-Hill School Division

Color Words

Write a color word to complete each sentence.

1. See the _____ fox.

red   pond   loud

2. _____ birds are beautiful.

Soft   Blue   There

3. The sky is _____ at night.

black   tall   what

4. The cat is _____.

hard   white   see

5. Grass is _____.

hot   like   green

Color Words

> • Some adjectives tell about colors.

> **Mechanics:**
> • Use an apostrophe (') in place of **o** in a contraction with <u>not</u>.

Look at each picture. Read the words next to it. Draw a circle around the color words. Color the picture as the sentence tells you to.

1. Color Pam's flowers red.

2. Color Tam's jacket blue.

3. Color Greg's hat green.

Write the sentence. Use a contraction for the underlined words.

Grass <u>is</u> <u>not</u> red.

_____

Number Words

- Some adjectives are words for numbers.

I	one
2	two
3	three
4	four
5	five

Read the sentences. Circle each number word.

I. Owl saw one mouse.

2. Owl saw two rabbits.

3. Four birds were in the tree.

4. Three rabbits saw Owl.

5. Five bats flew by.

EXTENSION: The children can write sentences with number words and exchange these sentences. Then they can find the number word in each other's sentences.

147

Number Words

- Some adjectives are words for numbers.
  Owl has <u>seven</u> brothers.

6 six

7 seven

8 eight

9 nine

10 ten

Read the sentences. Find the number words. Draw
a circle around each number word.

1. Do you have eight cats?

2. Nine cats are a lot.

3. Ten cats are too many cats.

4. Greg is seven years old.

5. I am six years old.

EXTENSION: Have each child write a sentence with a
number word. Then have them draw a number picture to go
with the sentence.

Book 1.5/Unit 1
Owl and the Moon   5

McGraw-Hill School Division

Number Words in Sentences

- Some adjectives are words for numbers.

  There are <u>ten</u> trees
  on my street.

Read the sentences. Circle the number words.
Draw what the sentence tells you.

1. Draw three owls.

2. Draw one moon in the sky.

3. Draw four furry pets.

4. Draw seven trees.

5. Draw ten flowers.

Correcting Sentences

> • The name of each day begins with a capital letter.

Read the sentences. Circle the correct way to write the days. Write the name of the day on the line.

1. Two friends have fun on _____.

   Saturday   saturday   sat.

2. We shopped in three stores on _____.

   monday   mon.   Monday

3. _____ was the day we picked ten apples.

   Wednesday   wed.   wednesday

4. We gathered six oranges on _____.

   tues.   Tuesday   tuesday

5. We went to buy six pears on _____.

   fri.   Friday   friday

McGraw-Hill School Division

Number Words

Read each sentence. Find the word that is a number word.

1. I have five ducks.

   (A) have   (B) ducks   (C) five

2. Owl looks at two bats.

   (A) two   (B) moons   (C) looks

3. Owl sees seven stars.

   (A) seven   (B) stars   (C) sees

4. Owl saw eight trees.

   (A) saw   (B) trees   (C) eight

5. Can you see the nine red trees?

   (A) trees   (B) you   (C) nine

Number Words

> • Some adjectives are words for numbers.

> **Mechanics:**
> • The name of each day begins with a capital letter.

Read each sentence aloud. Circle the adjective that tells how many.

I. I ate three cookies.

2. Tam saw ten ducks.

3. This Sunday I will be seven.

4. I have two cats.

5. There are eight trees on my street.

6. The cat has six kittens.

Write this sentence with the correct capital letters.

There are two games on saturday and sunday.

_____

_____

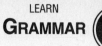

Synonyms

- Some words have meanings that are almost the same.

  These words are called **synonyms**.

  smile = grin

Look at each word in list A. One word in list B means almost the same. Draw a line to match the words that mean almost the same.

	A	**B**
I.	high	hop
2.	cut	tall
3.	big	funny
4.	jump	large
5.	silly	chop

McGraw-Hill School Division

EXTENSION: Have students act out words such as *look*, *write*, *run*, and *eat*. Have the class brainstorm words for the actions.

Antonyms

- Some words have meanings that are opposite.
- These words are called **antonyms**.

    big → small

Look at each word in list A. One word in list B means the opposite. Draw a line to match the words that mean the opposite.

	A	B
1.	night	down
2.	hot	soft
3.	in	day
4.	up	cold
5.	hard	out

154

EXTENSION: The children can read stories in their readers
to find antonyms. Make a list of antonym pairs they find.

Book 1.5/Unit 1
The Night Animals /5

McGraw-Hill School Division

Synonyms and Antonyms

- Some words have meanings that are almost the same.

    These words are called **synonyms**.

    hat = cap

- Some words have meanings that are opposite.

    These words are called **antonyms**.

    big → small

Look at the two underlined words. Circle S if the words are synonyms. Circle A if the words are antonyms.

1. The <u>night</u> is dark.   <u>day</u>   S   A

2. <u>Come</u> here.   <u>go</u>   S   A

3. He <u>jogs</u>.   <u>runs</u>   S   A

4. Look at my <u>hat</u>.   <u>cap</u>   S   A

5. He is <u>happy</u>.   <u>sad</u>   S   A

EXTENSION: Have children substitute the synonym or antonym for the underlined word in each of the above sentences. Ask them to read the new sentences aloud.

Capital Letters in Book Titles

> - The important words in a book title begin with a capital letter.
> - Draw a line under the title of a book.

Read the sentences about books. Circle titles that are correct.

1. <u>Night and Day Animals</u> is a good book.

2. <u>Curious george</u> is a book about a nosy monkey.

3. <u>Where the wild things Are</u> is not about tame places.

Write the wrong titles correctly on the lines below.

_____

_____

EXTENSION: Have the children look at books to see if the titles are capitalized correctly.

Book 1.5/Unit 1
The Night Animals 5

Synonyms and Antonyms

Read each sentence. Find the word that means the same as the underlined word. Write your answer on the line.

1. I am glad. _____

happy   old

2. The mouse is small. _____

kind   little

3. The girl is kind. _____

nice   mean

Read each sentence. Find the word that means the opposite of the underlined word. Write your answer on the line.

4. It is hot today. _____

cold   little

5. He went up. _____

here   down

Synonyms and Antonyms

- Some words have meanings that are almost the same.

  These words are called **synonyms**.

  jog = run

- Some words have meanings that are opposite.

  These words are called **antonyms**.

  cold ➔ hot

Read each sentence. Look at the underlined word.
Write the word that means almost the same.

1. She has a <u>hat</u>.　　_____

　　cap　　　silly

2. The rabbit can <u>hop</u>.　_____

　　jump　　　cut

Read each sentence. Look at the underlined word.
Write the word that means the opposite.

1. The cat is <u>big</u>.　　_____

　　small　　　fat

2. We went <u>in</u>.　　_____

　　cold　　　out

McGraw-Hill School Division

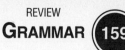
Adjectives

Choose the word that belongs in each space. Mark the letter for your answer.

What is that __(1)__ smell? That rose smells good.

    I. Ⓐ sweet   Ⓑ rose   Ⓒ are

Mike is tall. He is __(2)__ than Greg. Greg is smaller than Mike.

    2. Ⓐ small   Ⓑ taller   Ⓒ big

Pam is fast. She is faster than Kate and Tam. She is the __(3)__ of them all.

    3. Ⓐ fastest   Ⓑ faster   Ⓒ fast

The apple is red. The pear is __(4)__. The corn is yellow.

    4. Ⓐ pink   Ⓑ green   Ⓒ blue

I have two hands. I have __(5)__ fingers. My feet have ten toes.

    5. Ⓐ five   Ⓑ two   Ⓒ ten

Go on ➡

Adjectives

The grass is green. It is __(6)__ than the pear.

6. Ⓐ green   Ⓑ greener   Ⓒ greenest

The __(7)__ baby is crying. That baby is small.

7. Ⓐ little   Ⓑ tall   Ⓒ old

The stars are bright. The full moon is brighter. The sun is the __(8)__ of them all.

8. Ⓐ brightest   Ⓑ darkest   Ⓒ whitest

The owl is up in the tree. The skunk is __(9)__ below.

9. Ⓐ above   Ⓑ high   Ⓒ down

The cat is big. The dog is __(10)__ than the cat. The cow is the biggest of the three.

10. Ⓐ smaller   Ⓑ bigger   Ⓒ largest

Subjects

> - Sentences are made up of parts.
> - The subject tells *whom* or *what* the sentence is about.
>
> <u>Little Bear</u> lived alone.
>
> The sentence is about Little Bear.

Circle the subject in each sentence.

1. Little Bear is sad.

2. A stick comes floating by.

3. The bottle is filled with water.

4. A wooden horse runs around the island.

5. The island has no room.

5 Book 1.5/Unit 2
A Friend for Little Bear

EXTENSION: Have the children think of other subjects to complete each sentence.

161

Match the Sentence Parts

> - The subject tells *whom* or *what* the sentence is about.
>
>   <u>Little Bear</u> dances.
>
>   The subject is *Little Bear*.

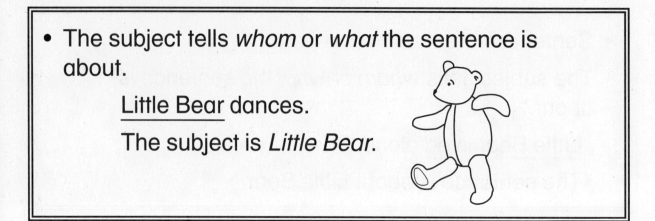

Look at the picture. Draw a line to match the parts of sentences about the picture.

	A	B
1.	Little Bear	is Little Bear's friend
2.	Owl	sits on a tree
3.	The cat	fills the bottle
4.	Frog	is sleeping
5.	The wooden horse	jumps

EXTENSION: Have the children write sentence subjects and exchange them. Then have them complete one another's sentences.

Book 1.5/Unit 2
A Friend for Little Bear

5

McGraw-Hill School Division

Write the Subject

> • The subject tells *whom* or *what* the sentence is about.
>
>   Little Bear draws pictures.

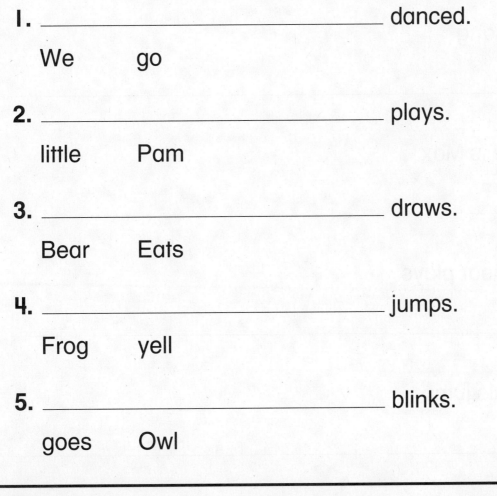

Read the sentences. Choose the word that would be the subject. Write it on the line.

1. _____ danced.

    We   go

2. _____ plays.

    little   Pam

3. _____ draws.

    Bear   Eats

4. _____ jumps.

    Frog   yell

5. _____ blinks.

    goes   Owl

5   Book 1.5/Unit 2
A Friend for Little Bear

EXTENSION: Read a trade book aloud to the children and have them listen for subjects.

163

Correcting Sentences

> • Begin every sentence with a capital letter.
>
> • End every sentence with a special mark.

Write each sentence. Begin with a capital letter.
End with a special mark.

1. the bird sings

_____

2. who sang

_____

3. where is Max

_____

4. little Bear plays

_____

5. animals jump

_____

EXTENSION: Have the children reread stories to find capital
letters at the beginning of sentences and to identify the
special mark at the end of the sentences.

Book 1.5/Unit 2
A Friend for Little Bear 5

McGraw-Hill School Division

Subjects

Circle the subject in each sentence.

1. Little Bear lives alone.

2. He needs a friend.

3. A stick comes floating by.

4. The wooden horse is a friend.

5. The island has no room.

6. The cat is sleeping.

7. The bird sings.

8. Frog jumps.

More Practice with Subjects

- Sentences are made up of parts.
- The subject tells *whom* or *what* the sentence is about.

Mechanics:

Begin every sentence with a capital letter.

Find the complete sentences. Write them correctly on the lines. Color the picture to match what the sentences say.

little Bear

little Bear is brown.

is brown.

his pail

his pail is red.

_____

_____

McGraw-Hill School Division

Predicates

> - Sentences are made up of parts.
> - The predicate tells what the subject does or is.
>
>   Silvia <u>tries on her shoes.</u>
>
>

Read each sentence. Circle the predicate.

1. A package arrives.

2. Silvia gets a present.

3. She has new shoes.

4. The shoes are red.

5. Silvia puts them on.

EXTENSION: Have the children write predicates and exchange them with a partner. Then have the children write subjects to go with the predicates.

Find the Predicate

- Sentences are made up of parts.
- The predicate tells what the subject does or is.

   Silvia <u>puts on her new shoes</u>.

Circle the predicate in each sentence.

1. Everyone likes new shoes.

2. Those shoes are red.

3. Silvia is happy.

4. My shoes fit.

5. Her shoes are too big.

EXTENSION: Read a trade book aloud and have the children listen for predicates.

Book 1.5/Unit 2
New Shoes for Silvia
 5

McGraw-Hill School Division

Matching Subjects and Predicates

> • The predicate tells what the subject does or is.

Use these predicates to complete the sentences below.

> helps Mama.
> fit.
> loves Silvia.

Write a predicate on the line to complete the sentence.

1. The shoes _____.

2. Mama _____.

3. Silvia _____.

Use these predicates to complete the sentences below.

> writes a letter
> talks to Rosa

Write a predicate on the line to complete the sentence.

1. Grandmother _____.

2. Mama _____.

McGraw-Hill School Division

5

Book 1.5/Unit 2

New Shoes for Silvia

EXTENSION: Have the children compose sentences about getting a new pair of shoes. Then have them circle the predicate.

169

Capital Letters for Holidays

> • The name of a holiday begins with a capital letter.

Write the name of the holiday correctly.

1. We like _____. new year's day

2. Mom likes _____. mother's day

3. When is _____? thanksgiving

4. We send cards on _____. valentine's day

5. Dad gets a gift on _____. father's day

EXTENSION: Have each child write a sentence about a holiday.

Book 1.5/Unit 2
New Shoes for Silvia
5

McGraw-Hill School Division

Test

Read each sentence. Find the predicate. Mark your answer.

1. The shoes are too big.

    Ⓐ shoes

    Ⓑ are too big

    Ⓒ shoes are

2. Mama wrote a letter.

    Ⓐ wrote a letter

    Ⓑ a letter

    Ⓒ Mama

3. I like red shoes.

    Ⓐ I

    Ⓑ I like

    Ⓒ like red shoes

4. These shoes fit.

    Ⓐ shoes

    Ⓑ fit

    Ⓒ These shoes

5. Silvia has new shoes.

    Ⓐ has new shoes

    Ⓑ Silvia has

    Ⓒ shoes

Predicates

- Sentences are made up of parts.
- The predicate tells what the subject does or is.

    The new red shoes <u>were too big</u>.

> **Mechanics:**
> The name of a holiday begins with a capital letter.

Read the words aloud. Write the words correctly in
a sentence. Underline the predicate. Circle the
capital letter in the name of holidays.

1. tried the shoes on. Silvia

_____

2. were too big. The shoes

_____

3. fit now. My shoes

_____

4. likes thanksgiving. Silvia

_____

5. were red. The shoes

_____

EXTENSION: Have the children find their favorite sentence in
the story "New Shoes for Silvia." Then have them circle the
predicate.

Pronouns

- A **pronoun** is a word that takes the place of a noun.
  He can take the place of a noun that names
  a boy or a man.

  Little Blue Bird grew. **He** grew fast.

  She can take the place of a noun that names
  a girl or a woman.

  Little Blue Bird's sister can fly. **She** can fly.

  It can take the place of a noun that names a thing.

  The book tells about birds. **It** tells about birds.

Read the sentences. Find the underlined nouns. Write a pronoun on the line to replace the underlined nouns.

| **Pronouns:** | He | She | It |

1. Tim has a bird. _____

2. Pam has a cat. _____

3. Mom wrote my name. _____

4. The tree was a tall oak. _____

5. My sister is big. _____

McGraw-Hill School Division

 Book 1.5/Unit 2
The Story of a Bluebird

EXTENSION: Have each student write a sentence. Then have students exchange sentences with a partner. The partner should replace the noun with a pronoun.

Write the Pronoun

> • A **pronoun** is a word that takes the place of a noun.
> *They* can take the place of a plural noun.
> > The birds flew home.
> > *They* flew home.
> *They* can also take the place
> of more than one noun.
> > Birds and bats can fly high.
> > *They* can fly high.

Read the sentences. Write a pronoun for each underlined part.

Pronouns:	He	She	It	They

1. The girl waved at us. _____

2. The boys jumped high. _____

3. Frogs and toads like bugs. _____

4. Boys and girls go to school. _____

5. Some children like to swing. _____

McGraw-Hill School Division

EXTENSION: Have the children write sentences with a plural subject. Then have them exchange sentences with a partner. The partner should replace the subject with a pronoun.

Book 1.5/Unit 2
The Story of a Bluebird

Choose a Pronoun

> • A pronoun is a word that takes the place
> of a noun.

Write the pronoun for each underlined part of the
sentence.

| He | She | It | They |

1. <u>Mother</u> helps her children. _____

2. <u>My brother</u> is little. _____

3. <u>Mom and Dad</u> pack the van. _____

4. <u>The birds</u> flew by. _____

5. <u>The van</u> is red. _____

EXTENSION: Have the children write a sentence with a
pronoun. Then have them draw a picture to show who or
what the pronoun refers to.

Using Commas

- Use a comma between the day and year in a date.
- Use a comma between the name of a city and a state.
- Use a comma after the greeting in a letter.
- Use a comma after the closing in a letter.

Read the parts of a letter. Write a comma where it is needed.

1. Dear Pam

2. You asked me about Little Blue Bird on May 2 2000.

3. Little Blue Bird lives in Center City Indiana.

4. His birthday is March 27 1999.

5. He wants to fly to Gary Indiana.

6. Your friend

   Tim

176

EXTENSION: Have students write their own letters. Tell them to circle the commas.

Book 1.5/Unit 2
The Story of a Bluebird
6

McGraw-Hill School Division

Pronouns

Read each sentence. Write the pronoun on the line.

1. He can fly. _____

2. She helps people. _____

3. They looked here. _____

4. It was a nest. _____

5. They are blue birds. _____

Pronouns

> • A pronoun is a word that takes the place of a noun.

Mechanics:
- Use a comma between the day and year in a date.
- Use a comma between the name of a city and a state.
- Use a comma after the greeting in a letter.
- Use a comma after the closing in a letter.

Look at each picture. Read the words next to them. Write a pronoun for the underlined words. Write a comma where it is needed.

1. The <u>girls</u> were born on May 27 1998.

_____

2. <u>Rosa</u> lives in Dallas Texas.

_____

3. Dear Pam
   I saw your cat.
   <u>Your cat</u> is big. _____
   Your friend
   Tim

McGraw-Hill School Division

I and *Me*

- The word *I* is used in the subject of a sentence.

  <u>I</u> am glad to see you.

Write the pronoun *I* on the line.

I. _____ like Amelia.

2. Pam and _____ want to fly.

3. _____ must learn to fly.

4. Tim and _____ flew in a plane.

5. _____ will fly today.

5 Book 1.5/Unit 2
Young Amelia Earhart

EXTENSION: The children can write sentences beginning with *I* and telling about a person they look up to.

179

McGraw-Hill School Division

Writing *Me*

- *I* and *me* are pronouns.
- The word *me* is used in the predicate of a sentence.

    Dad gave *me* a book.

Write the pronoun *me* on the line.

1. Will you please give _____ the book?

2. Pam came with _____.

3. Mom reads the book to _____.

4. She helped _____.

5. Tim gave _____ a book.

EXTENSION: Have children write a sentence that has <u>me</u> in it. Then they can draw a picture of "me" doing what the sentence says to do.

Book 1.5/Unit 2
Young Amelia Earhart 5

Choosing *I* or *Me*

> - *I* and *me* are pronouns.
> - The word *I* is used in the subject of a sentence.
> - The word *me* is used in the predicate of a sentence.

Write the correct pronoun. Use *I* or *me*.

1. _____ like to read.

2. Please read it to _____.

3. Pam and _____ can read.

4. Tim gave _____ a toy plane.

5. _____ gave Tim the book.

5 Book 1.5/Unit 2
Young Amelia Earhart

EXTENSION: Have students read sentences in the story, substituting *I* and *me* for subject and object nouns.

181

The Pronoun *I*

> • The pronoun *I* is always a capital letter.
>
>   **I** can play games.

Read the sentences. Find the pronoun *I*. Look to see if it is written correctly. Change the incorrect I's to correct ones.

1. i am in first grade.

_____

2. Greg and I will walk in the rain.

_____

3. Pam and i are friends.

_____

4. I can jump very high.

_____

5. i like to play ball with my friends.

_____

EXTENSION: The children can write sentences with *I* as a subject. Then they can proofread to be sure they have made all of the *I*'s capital letters.

Book 1.5/Unit 2
Young Amelia Earhart   5

Using *I* and *Me*

Choose the correct pronoun. Mark your answer.

1. Amelia Earhart is a hero to _____.

Ⓐ I   Ⓑ me   Ⓒ he

2. _____ am lucky.

Ⓐ I   Ⓑ me   Ⓒ he

3. Amelia played baseball like _____.

Ⓐ I   Ⓑ me   Ⓒ he

4. _____ will learn about planes.

Ⓐ I   Ⓑ me   Ⓒ it

5. Tell _____ about Amelia.

Ⓐ I   Ⓑ me   Ⓒ he

Using *I* and *Me*

> - *I* and *me* are pronouns.
> - The word *I* is used in the subject of a sentence.

Mechanics:

The pronoun *I* is always a capital letter.

Read each sentence aloud. Put an *I* or *me* where they belong.

1. _____ will learn to fly.

2. _____ will fly some day.

3. Will you fly with _____?

4. _____ will read about planes.

5. You can tell _____ about the plane.

Combining Sentences

> • Parts of two sentences are sometimes the same.
> • You can use <u>and</u> to make two sentences into one.
>   Pam <u>likes flying</u>. Greg <u>likes flying</u>.
>   Pam <u>and</u> Greg like flying.

Read these sentences. Write <u>and</u> on the line to make two sentences into one.

1. Pam reads books.

Tim reads books.

Pam _____ Tim read books.

2. Cars carry people.

Ships carry people.

Cars _____ ships carry people.

3. Ships move on water.

Boats move on water.

Ships _____ boats move on water.

4. Tam likes ducks.

Tim likes ducks.

Tam _____ Tim like ducks.

---

4 Book 1.5/Unit 2
On the Go!

EXTENSION: Have the children write sentences with their names and classmates' names and join the names with <u>and</u>.

Combining Sentences

> • Parts of two sentences are sometimes the same.
> • You can use <u>and</u> to make two sentences into one.

Use <u>and</u> to make the two sentences into one. Write
the new sentence.

I. I read.

  I write.

  I _____

2. The frog jumps.

  The frog bumps.

  The frog _____

3. Pam hits.

  Pam runs.

  Pam _____

4. The ducks eat.

  The ducks sleep.

  The ducks _____

EXTENSION: Have the children look in their readers for
sentences that can be joined with <u>and</u>.

Book 1.5/Unit 2
On the Go! /4

McGraw-Hill School Division

Combining Sentences

> • Parts of two sentences are sometimes the same.
> • You can use <u>and</u> to make two sentences into one.

Read the sentences. Draw a circle around the parts that can be joined by <u>and</u>. Write the new sentence.

1. Pam likes reading. Pam likes writing.

_____

2. Tam has a duck. Tam has a cat.

_____

3. Max plays. Max eats.

_____

4. Trucks go on land. Trains go on land.

_____

5. People ride in cars. People fly in planes.

_____

McGraw-Hill School Division

5 Book 1.5/Unit 2
On the Go!

EXTENSION: Have the children work in pairs. Each can write a simple sentence. Then they can work together to join the sentences with <u>and</u>.

Using Capital Letters

> • The pronoun *I* is always a capital letter.
>
> • A proper noun begins with a capital letter.

Read the sentences. Circle the pronoun *I* where it should be a capital. Circle proper nouns to show they should be capital.

1. i can ride a bus to green school.

2. Greg goes in a car to pine school.

3. Amelia flew an airplane to new york.

4. i like to ride trains.

5. Trucks can carry things to chicago.

6. pam is my friend.

McGraw-Hill School Division

EXTENSION: Have students write sentences about where they live. Tell them to circle the capital letters.

Test

Combine each pair of sentences. Write the new sentence on the line.

1. I like ice cream.

I like cake.

_____

2. Greg has a birthday in June.

Mike has a birthday in June.

_____

3. Mike has a pet cat.

Mike has a pet gerbil.

_____

4. My friends help me.

My friends work with me.

_____

5. Saturday is a special day.

Sunday is a special day.

_____

Combining Sentences

- Parts of two sentences are sometimes the same.
- You can use <u>and</u> to make two sentences into one.

Mechanics:
- The pronoun *I* is always a capital letter.
- A proper noun begins with a capital letter.

Circle the letters that should be capital letters. Use <u>and</u> to make two sentences into one. Write the new sentences.

I. i fly to Ohio.   You fly to ohio.

_____

2. Trucks go on land.   Trains go on land.

_____

3. i go by car.   i go by plane.

_____

4. tam goes to dallas.   max goes to dallas.

_____

5. mom helps me read.   mom helps me write.

_____

McGraw-Hill School Division

Book 1.5/Unit 2
On the Go!   5

More About Sentences

Read the sentences in the box. Look at the part with the line under it. Which is the better way to say this part? Mark your answer.

> Little Bear lives on an island. Little Bear is lonely. <u>Needs a friend.</u>
> (1)

1. Ⓐ A friend needs.
   Ⓑ Little Bear needs a friend.
   Ⓒ Needs friend Little Bear.

> Silvia had new red shoes. <u>The shoes was a gift</u>. The shoes fit.
> (2)

2. Ⓐ The shoes were a gift.
   Ⓑ The shoes a gift.
   Ⓒ A gift the shoes.

> The little bluebird grew wings. <u>Learned to fly</u>. It went away.
> (3)

3. Ⓐ Wings to fly.
   Ⓑ They learned to fly.
   Ⓒ It learned to fly.

> Pam sees the sad cat. She is sad. <u>Hugs the cat.</u>
> (4)

4. Ⓐ She hugs the cat.
   Ⓑ It hugs the cat.
   Ⓒ He hugs the cat.

Go on

I like Amelia. <u>Tell I about Amelia.</u> How did she learn to fly?
(5)

5. Ⓐ Tell it about Amelia.
Ⓑ Tell me about Amelia.
Ⓒ Tell her about Amelia.

People go to places. <u>They walk. They ride cars.</u>
(6)

6. Ⓐ They walk cars.
Ⓑ They walk ride cars.
Ⓒ They walk and ride cars.

<u>I like to go places. He likes to go places.</u> We like to walk.
(7)

7. Ⓐ He and I like to go places.
Ⓑ He and me like to go places.
Ⓒ I and him like to go places.

We went to the store. <u>We saw big toys. We saw little toys.</u>
(8)

8. Ⓐ We saw toys.
Ⓑ We saw big little toys.
Ⓒ We saw big and little toys.